GLASGOW

A · CELEBRATION

EDITED BY CLIFF HANLEY

WITH PHOTOGRAPHS BY
OSCAR MARZAROLI

MAINSTREAM
PUBLISHING

First published in 1984 by
MAINSTREAM PUBLISHING,
7 Albany Street, Edinburgh, EH1 3UG.

ISBN 0 906391 75 X

Typeset in 11 point Garamond by Studioscope
in conjunction with Mainstream Publishing.

Printed in Great Britain by
McCorquadale (Scotland) Ltd., Glasgow.

GLASGOW—A CELEBRATION

CONTENTS

CONTRIBUTORS

IAN ARCHER, who can write literately about football, is also outstanding among sports journalists for the range of his interests. He is an Oxford graduate in law.

CLEM ASHBY, Shakespearean to trade, became one of Scotland's best-loved TV newsreaders. Also a fiendish crossword solver.

JOE BELTRAMI stands in a great tradition of Glasgow lawyers who bring wit as well as wisdom to court.

EDDIE BOYD probably has the longest as well as the most distinguished track record in Scotland as a radio and television writer, though he was raised in a town where children were produced solely to work in a dynamite factory.

JANEY BUCHAN, former Communist, former Glasgow Councillor, and always ready to speak her mind, is now Glasgow's MEP.

JOHN BURROWES, deputy editor of the Daily Record, *is also author of several big-selling books, notably his work on Benny Lynch,* Benny: The Life and Times of a Fighting Legend. *He doesn't like boxing.*

DEIRDRE CHAPMAN, Carnoustie-born, started as a Glasgow journalist in her teens on the now vanished Evening News. *She has also revealed a powerful gift as a short story writer.*

CHRISTIAN CIVARDI is a Frenchman. Echoes of the Auld Alliance sing through his writings on Scotland. M. Civardi's book Ecosse *(1980), was brought to our attention by Pat Woods.*

EMILIO COIA was the youngest student ever to be admitted to Glasgow School of Art, has caricatured the great and the small and is also a journalist.

BILLY CONNOLLY was the first man to make the English understand Glesca humour. His contribution is taken from the album Billy Connolly Solo Concert *(Transatlantic Records Ltd.).*

JAMES COPLAND, actor, painter, poet and philosopher, has found inspirations for all four careers in his native city.

LAVINIA DERWENT, the lassie from the Borders, has had her children's books translated into a score of languages, two of them have been dramatised for television, and her continuing autobiography is a continuing delight.

JAMES DONNELLY, *now with the* Sunday Express, *was one of the most exuberant writers in the old* Evening Citizen *25 years ago. The exuberance has increased.*

FRASER ELDER, *the Dundonian immigrant, writes quiz books on the side, works as a sports journalist in all available media, and holds that Dundee people imagine they are living in* The Broons.

ALEX FRUTIN, *tidily into his eighties, was one of the best-loved theatrical magnates of Glasgow, and still is.*

RIKKI FULTON, *a Children's Hour actor as a child, graduated to comedy on television and on stage. In recent years he has moved easily into classical roles and still has some surprises in store for us.*

RAYMOND GARDNER, *among other things "Trencherman" of the* Glasgow Herald, *eats prodigiously and remains preternaturally thin. It has something to do with metabolism and wine connoisseurship.*

ALASDAIR GRAY, *the totally outrageous Alasdair Gray, artist and author, cannot be described, but Anthony Burgess classes him as the Scottish writer of the century, which is not bad. His short story first appeared in* Unlikely Stories, Mostly *published by Canongate (1984).*

ROBIN HALL, *for years a partner with Jimmy McGregor in the most successful folk duo of their time, still plays and sings but has settled into presenting much-loved musical programmes on BBC Scotland.*

DR GEORG HEUSER, *Director of the Goethe Institute in Scotland, had a long-standing fascination for Glasgow before he even saw it, and now that he has, remains captivated in wide-eyed wonder.*

HAMISH IMLACH, *born in India, had to learn about Scotland the hard way, but triumphed, and even as a folk-singer he is a man without an enemy.*

DR MICHAEL KELLY *has certainly been Glasgow's most visible and ubiquitous Lord Provost, in a town which has had many theatrical heads. He is remembered at the moment for his Glasgow's Miles Better crusade, but has a new career ahead in business and TV journalism.*

TOM LEONARD *is one of the New Wave of Glasgow poets, now quite grown up, who has thrawnly insisted that Glasgow topics, and the Glasgow tongue, are the only true stuff of great literature.*

LIZ LOCHHEAD *wrote, and writes, funny poems but is now deeply engaged in theatre both as dramatist and performer. Her enthusiastic feminism does not exclude men from the human race.*

SHERIFF ANDREW LOTHIAN, *the most genial of judges, is equally devoted to law and literature, and is active in International P.E.N.*

BET LOW *is one of Scotland's most successful painters, despite being married to Tom McDonald, another of Scotland's most successful painters. They are a happy team working as individuals.*

BASHIR MAAN, *Glasgow's first Pakistani Town Councillor, is the non-local boy made good, now in warehousing and ceaselessly active in Labour politics. His golf is highly variable.*

RANALD McCOLL *is too young to have drunk fully the rich potion of Bud Neill's contribution to Glasgow's consciousness, since he was at school with the editor's son. But being mesmerised, he is working on the definitive book on the immortal Bud.*

CARL MacDOUGALL'S *most performed work is* Cod Liver Oil, *reprinted here among other things. He wrote it as a parody on a reverent song about Wise men from the East. The original has since sunk without trace under the weight.*

AGNES McLEAN, *the beloved firebrand, is probably the most intensely Glaswegian phenomenon in the city. Lifelong radical, trade union organiser, she is now a Strathclyde Regional Councillor.*

WILLIAM McILVANNEY *is a Protean talent in verse, short story and novel. His realistic police tale* Laidlaw *is one of the literary events of the generation. His contribution to this book first appeared in* Scottish International *in 1973.*

EBENEZER McILWHAM, *the bard of Whifflet West, is an enigmatic octogenarian who was rumoured to have written his early works on walls, for durability. But since he is a peripatetic recluse, little more can be revealed.*

EDWIN MORGAN *teaches at university level and writes to people on every level . . . not quite all people, it turns out.*

STEPHEN MULRINE *teaches at Glasgow School of Art, produced a solid body of Glasgow poetry when the mood took him, but is now devoted to work for the theatre. he conducts a popular writers' workshop on radio.*

OWEN O'LEARY *was a teacher of English in Glasgow, and in his retirement realised that he had been bored senseless analysing other men's writings. He is spending his twilight years getting his own back.*

JIMMY REID came into prominence during the John Brown Shipyard sit-in, went on to become a distinguished Lord Rector of Glasgow University, is now a full-time journalist writing in the Daily Record *and elsewhere.*

CRAIG SAMET describes his own career. This sharp-eyed Chicagoan is editor of the successful marketing magazine, Presentation.

BILLY SLOAN, pop writer with the Daily Record, *was born in Rottenrow, brought up in Martyr Street, Townhead, worked on a Corporation building site before journalism, and presents the "new music" show on Radio Clyde. He once met a guy who was in the same class as Lulu.*

NORMAN WHITE, Cheshire-born, is a bass baritone with Scottish Opera, a tireless organiser of fund-rasing events for the company, and an adoptive Glaswegian of seventeen years standing.

RUTH WISHART is one of Scotland's toughest journalists in the very best sense. With many other talented hacks she went down with the foundered Sunday Standard *but surfaced at once and is now writing regularly for* The Observer, The Scotsman *and other grateful heavies.*

CHRIS YOUNG describes himself as the ageing vocalist, though he doesn't look it, spends his summers presenting and performing in cabaret in Ayr, and pursues his obsession with old Glasgow music hall, on which he is now completing an entire book.

OSCAR MARZAROLI was born in Italy and didn't even become naturalised until his twenties; but then went as far as attending the Kirk. He is a film producer and director of repute, but the still camera is his wildest delight. He has snapped brilliantly in several European countries and lovingly in the Highlands as well as recording Glasgow for decades. He is peerless.

WHAT'S TO CELEBRATE?

Cliff Hanley

OF THE MAKING of many books about Glasgow there is no end. This is not an apology, it is simply a fact. The same thing applies to songs. Offhand I can think of two songs about Edinburgh, a city which I much admire: "Within a Mile o' Edinburgh Toon" and "The Bonnie Wells o' Wearie", which is guaranteed to bring on the rain. Glasgow has inspired scores of songs, including the drunkard's international anthem, "I Belong to Glasgow". I have written over a dozen myself, lost to all sense of shame or decency.

Why do we bother? The place, as is well known all over the world, is a grimy swamp of drink and violence, deprivation and anarchy.

It is hypnotic, that's why. My own first published book, *Dancing in the Streets*, written half-reluctantly at the behest of a Renfrew man then living in London, was, I thought, an intensely boring recollection of the most ordinary childhood in the world. I had grown up in the vanished Gallowgate in what I thought was the most ordinary family in existence, because it was mine. I had not run away to sea at ten. I had never been swept off my feet in early teens by a beautiful, nymphomaniac, rich White Russian countess. There was a fearful shortage of White Russian countesses in the Gallowgate, and there wasn't much bread about either. I was so ordinary I was ashamed.

When that book rushed into four impressions inside a year, my view of the universe was shattered. My intention had been to explain the quiddity, the whatness, of this perfectly mundane city to strangers—my notional reader was an unfrocked Buddhist priest in Ulan Bator.

Don't know how well it went in Ulan Bator, they never gave me a breakdown. It did go a bomb in Glasgow, and later in Liverpool and Newcastle and other such dull ordinary cities, because I had done something totally unintentional. I had given people back their childhood. It had not occurred to me while I was writing this trivial reminiscence, that people *forget*, and the principal talent that went into that book was total recall.

I remembered everything that had happened to me, from the age of two or earlier, and just told it the way it was. People of my own generation screamed in recognition—"Yes, that was me too," they screamed.

If I had been raised on a sampan on the Yangtse, and learned to read and write, I would have written the same kind of book, if a Renfrew man in London had asked me. And it might have roused the same response, because there is a universal quality in the wonderings and wanderings of childhood. Years ago I heard a wireless programme about childhood games, by a dogged sociologist guy who had searched the world for them, and he reported that they were all international at bottom, except for one game played exclusively in the Loop district of Chicago. He went on to describe this pointless exercise, and I leapt from my chair shouting, "It's Hunch Cuddy Hunch!"

So, in a big way, the Glasgow experience is the world experience. But the town still has a quiddity, a whatness, a uniqueness. Look at the words of the Frenchman Christian Civardi in this book, you don't have to accept my word. I am obviously prejudiced, and aim to remain so.

Glasgow was a salmon-fishing village on the banks of the limpid Clyde, which provided St Kentigern with one of his best tricks. It developed bits of trade and expanded eastwards so that the Calton Weavers could go down in history as pioneer proletarian martyrs. It caught on to tobacco and some people got rich, just in time for a war across the Atlantic which put the kybosh on that. So it went into cotton, and the same thing happened again.

Virtually every trade or industry Glasgow got into, in fact, was due for extinction in no time. Iron, steel, the heavy stuff, shipbuilding—crazy, that, by the way. If shipbuilding were invented tomorrow, nobody would dream of doing it on the shallow little Clyde. I was once on the deck of an oil tanker being launched from John Brown's, trembling with heroism and working a camera, as it was released into this ludicrously narrow channel, and it was trailing hundreds of tons of drag-chains to discourage it from running up the main street in Renfrew. Insane. But Glasgow built ships because people wanted ships.

Oh, the wild mad pride of being the cradle of the Industrial Revolution! What that meant was sucking in the teeming masses from the Highlands and the Lowlands and Ireland to stuff them in dark satanic mills and deafening yards, and cram them into noisome tenements to spawn wee toty Glaswegians whose known world was a back court and a stairhead cludgy.

The industrial greatness of Glasgow was a grim and grubby greatness, and you could lean a ladder against the atmosphere, if the ladder was acid-proof. But it was a greatness all the same, and Clyde-built meant something round the globe.

And the regular hard times produced their defence mechanism, called the Glaswegian, who survived on *gemutlichkeit* and the joke. Booze too, of course. But mostly the joke. Practically every Scotch comic is a Glasgow comic and always has been, and he is merely the professional version of the keelie in the street.

Ah seen a murder in the chip-shoap
A wee dug stole a haddie-bone
A big dug tried tae take it aff it
So ah hut it wi' a tottie scone

Last night ah went tae ma Auntie Sarah's
Ma Auntie Sarah wisnae in
So ah keeked through a hole in the curtain
And ye'll never guess whit ah seen

Her teeth were lyin' on the table
Her hair was lyin' on the bed
An' ah couldnae help fae laughing
When ah saw her skewin' aff her widden leg

Early in life we learned the Meaning of Meaninglessness. We died of tuberculosis, we collapsed in gutters, and all the time we enjoyed the great joke. David Hume would have understood.

And we wrote books. Natives wrote books, incomers like Neil Munro wrote books, I wrote books, everybody wrote books. The sheer improbable wonder of the place drove people to pen and paper. My own collection of Glasgow books is twenty feet long and goes back centuries. I have plundered a few of them for this book.

How could you ever emigrate, I was asked plaintively when I left for a year in Canada. Easy. I took Glasgow with me in the bone marrow, and I was battered stupid by the number of Glaswegians I met there. After twenty years, some of them had thicker East End accents than mine. They were dogged bits of Glasgow converting a foreign field. I had been warned that you couldn't throw a brick in Yonge Street, Toronto, without hitting three keelies, so I took my own brick. The first guy it hit stole it, and I knew I was at home.

Oh, the hard times, and some of them were self-inflicted. We didn't exactly invent administrative vandalism, and I'm very glad I don't live in Liverpool where they still believe that if you don't live in a Corporation house you're some kind of fink; but we made a fair showing at the trade, scattering the old tenements and

Cliff who?

decanting decent Glasgow scruff into heartless suburban sprawls or battery-hen skyscrapers.

We learn, though, we learn, and we *even* learn that a city is a place for people to live in. It begins to look not too rotten.

When a London literary agent asked me peevishly why I kept writing books set in Glasgow, I had to explain that a man introduced to the magic of life by a raddled but cunning old strumpet was spoiled forever for vapid young maidens. That shut him up. Mind you, he was the kind of Southerner who cancelled a holiday in Argyll because he had heard about a typhoid epidemic in Aberdeen.

I must pause my muse. This book is for other people to write. When my Edinburgh publishers incited me to do this thing (I never have any ideas of my own) I realised something else about Glasgow. Practically everybody I was going to ask to contribute was a personal friend. I had never looked for a long list of personal friends. They happened in this strange, bewildered, totally annealed city. I love them all.

Interesting thing. Many of the totally uncritical, the totally besotted Glasgow pieces here are offered by the incomers, from the Borders or Pakistan or Germany, who don't see the blemishes so glaring to us natives. It has to mean something— they have standards of comparison.

I have to single out the magical Oscar Marzaroli, who was born in Italy and didn't even think of taking out British papers till his twenties. As well as being maybe the nicest Glaswegian at large (along with my other contributors, let it be said), he has the true eye of the lover, which finds beauty even in the blemishes, and you are lucky to have him. So am I.

Let us now praise famous men, and our fathers that begat us. And let us celebrate the grim, grey, gory, glorious, gorgeous Glasgow that hath made mortal life a hilarity on earth.

TREES AND FISH AND SUCHLIKE

D. Macleod Malloch

THE ARMORIAL INSIGNIA of Glasgow are richly storied, the emblems referring to several legends in the life of St Kentigern, who was the first bishop of Glasgow and died about AD 602. A tree represents the bough which, according to the old story, St Kentigern kindled by his word into a blaze in order to relight the church lights, which some of his enemies had put out. The bird perched upon the tree is a robin, the pet of St Serf, which St Kentigern restored to life, as the tradition goes. The bell which hangs upon the tree signifies the Church and See of Glasgow founded by St Kentigern.

But the most romantic legend of all is associated with the salmon, which bears a ring in its mouth. Tradition relates that the Queen of Cadzow had given away to a certain knight a ring which she had received as a present from her husband. The king, suspecting this, and being very wroth at such faithless conduct, considered how he might best discover her guilt and punish it.

One day when the king and his Court were out hunting along the banks of the Clyde, the knight to whom the queen had given the ring, overcome with fatigue, fell asleep under the shelter of a tree. The king seized the opportunity to look into the knight's pouch, and there, as he expected, he found the ring. Incensed beyond measure that the queen should have thus lightly treated the ring he gave her, he flung it into the river.

Returning home, he demanded the ring from the queen; at the same time telling her that she should be put to death if it was not produced. She immediately sent her maid to the knight to ask for it; but, of course, he could not find it. The queen knew not which way to turn. At last, in her despair, she besought herself of the good Bishop Kentigern. She avowed her fault to him, and expressed her sorrow and besought his advice and help.

The good man believed in her sincerity and took compassion upon her. He immediately sent one of his people to fish in the river, with instructions to bring him the first fish he caught. The angler soon returned and laid a huge salmon at the feet of the Bishop, who took from its mouth the very ring which the king had flung into the Clyde. The queen, receiving the ring from the Bishop, together with his blessing, hastened to take it home to her husband, and thus her life was saved by the good Bishop Kentigern.

The Book of Glasgow Anecdote

THE FOREIGN CITY

Deirdre Chapman

MY THEN four-year-old, home from Hillhead Primary 1, said, "Today the Russian children went upstairs to learn French."

French, English, does it matter? This is Glasgow. And Russian is a nice Glasgow collective noun for a mixed group of Indians, Pakistanis, Chinese and Chileans, suggesting global spread without nit-picking attention to physical and cultural detail.

Glasgow is a foreign city. Wherever you come from, there are always more people who have come from somewhere else. Never getting into a majority, nobody gets up enough steam to make rules. A pattern of life evolves that shifts with expediency, and precision of speech is never as much admired as is the happy knack of putting over what you mean, and more, while saying something else altogether. Only one thing is demanded of you if you stay here. If you're not nice already, you'd better learn to be.

It is a constant strain and depletion of the body's resources to be worrying all the time about appearances, and Edinburgh people are often quite worn out by it, feeling as they do that they are the heirs of history, custodians of its ruins and actors on one of its vacated lots. Consistency bothers them a lot . . . what colour to paint a New Town front door, what to wear to suggest you are a freewheeling citizen of the world and not a solid burgher . . . that sort of thing.

Glasgow people, on the other hand, have no common past, no group standards to defend, and little interest in facades. This leaves them with a great deal of excess energy which they lay down as "niceness".

Niceness hangs like fat about the Glasgow body and is drawn upon in all surprising and demanding situations or where no more appropriate response comes to mind. You may insult or otherwise damage a Glaswegian and still find him nice. Being nice gives him time to think. It also gives you time to think and you should use it. Niceness is a primary reaction, and while an astonishing number of Glaswegians have niceness all the way through like letters in a stick of rock (though not, of course, Edinburgh rock which is blank and tasteless even underneath), others have normal follow-up reactions. It should also be remembered that niceness can be cancelled out by alcohol and/or an underlying grievance. Having one's goodwill constantly mistaken for gullibility is an example of a grievance.

To a jaundiced observer, being nice to strangers could be written off as display if it were not that Glaswegians (with the foregoing exceptions) are inordinately nice to one another and can be heard everywhere checking on their companions' mental and physical wellbeing . . . "Y'awright Isa?" . . . "Y'OK Jimmy?".

Having lived in Glasgow for thirty years I am quite nice too, much nicer, I'm sure, than if I'd stayed on the East Coast where I belong. Since niceness induces a certain mental flabbiness, I can't recall the details of East Coast prejudice against Glaswegians, only that it seems in retrospect to have been based on unconscious racial prejudice. People in the east, Lowland Scots to a man, disliked and feared extrovert alien behaviour in what they thought were kinsmen. Kinsmen they are not.

All I knew about Glaswegians before I came here was that they were socially inferior. No one had actually spelled this out to me, but it was implicit in the drawing back of tweed skirts when Glaswegians invaded our small but tasteful golf and seaside resort during the Fair Fortnight. They spoke too loudly, laughed too much, wore the wrong colours together, and altogether the wrong clothes for putting. The entire population of Glasgow was working-class, I gathered, where we of the East were impeccably middle, regardless of individual circumstance. Of course they couldn't help that, but they might have done something about their voices.

The trouble was that they were impervious to criticism, utterly without self-consciousness, let their children run wild, ate fish and chips in the street, and thought the Medal Course was something like the Big Dipper, you just paid your money and walked on, eating your choc-ice.

Breughel at Bingham's

In the winter when they weren't there, their voices dominated the radio, from the refined provincial cosiness of Auntie Kathleen to the crowing West-slanted football commentaries that made my father's favourite winter sport hating Celtic and Rangers equally. In retrospect, my parents spent every Saturday evening running down Glaswegians, because that was the night the McFlannels were on too. They would never have been so unkind about foreigners, and the couple of times a coloured person visited the town, they were charming. They simply didn't realise that Glaswegians were foreigners, nor, then, did I.

When I got here in the fifties, my landlady was Italian and her maid-of-all-work Irish. There were wayside shrines all over the landings and stairs and they went to Mass before I was up. In the east I had never knowingly met a Catholic, and in history and geography classes at school I had had problems believing that Highlanders and Islanders were fellow-countrymen. Such wild tragedy and exotic scenery had no place in the tidy controlled environment I knew. But here were girls with names like Donalda who could sing in Gaelic and had aunties on Barra. And other girls in cashmere twinsets who lived in remote suburbs and had grandfathers who were Russian Jews.

All of these people spoke variations of the Glasgow accent, and all of them, however established, had the sort of personal transience and social curiosity you find nowadays mainly among American graduates back-packing round Europe.

If you're a stranger here, you're a stranger amongst strangers. So light is the hold on time and place that everyone can spot a lost traveller or disoriented lorry driver by simple identification. A neat, late, flustered job interviewee hunting for street numbers will be taken there and told on the way they're a lousy firm to work for. You have only to stand in an empty bus shelter looking vague and vulnerable for someone to come and put you right. "It's an awful service, where are you going? You'd be better with the 25, I'm going that way myself."

There is a kind and chaotic sloppiness about Glasgow which I can see must infuriate more orderly people. No one becomes totally identified with his or her job role—glamorous receptionist, relentless traffic warden, macho building worker—but keeps a wee amateur brain cell on the side, ready to assert itself if the job becomes ridiculous.

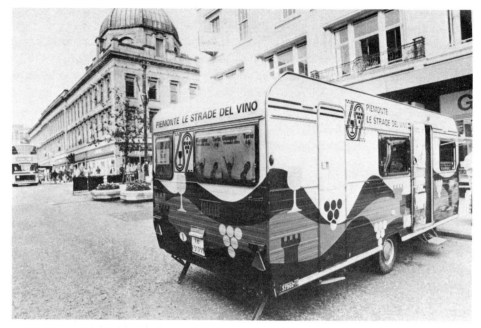

The Italians have landed

We have at the moment sixteen macho building workers on top of five sets of scaffolding within conversational range of our back garden, there being a long dry spell and bits of Glasgow always being under repair. They arrived acting the part of dynamic tradesmen, but have plainly come to live on the roofs for a few weeks or months, however long it takes. They took a few days to suss out the ambience. Tried a few macho howls. To a passing girl in a backless dress, "Aw hen, y'eve pit it oan back tae front." To the kids experimentally dismantling the scaffolding from below, "See you awa'r ah'll bile ye'n'ile." "Yehavenae goat ony ile." "Naw but the wummin has. Sunflower ile."

Now they are quite at home and sing strange bursts of Flamenco as a reflex every time the sun comes out. Glaswegians do not wrestle with their problems in silence and the building workers are having a lot of problems, technical and personal. They send someone on another roof out for lunch, "Jackie J'awannanurra Tizer'n'Quavers?" and settle back to ponder upon their sex lives, or their bowels. "Ah'm fuckin' regular ah can tell ye wance a fuckin' month."

They do not do it to annoy as they might in another town, but in their certainty that everyone in Glasgow enjoys a roof-top cabaret. We do, but perhaps the time has come to take it out of the private sector and put it on the rates.

I don't think I meant to stay here, but Glasgow is an easy place to live in and a hard place to leave. Gratuitous bitchiness is rare (unless as a joke, which excuses everything) so you shed whatever protective layer you brought with you, never get round to replacing it, and can be terribly wounded by a casual jibe on a trip to Edinburgh or London.

What structure we lack is provided from time to time by whatever immigrant community is currently influential. My youngest son, now in Primary 7, was very sure that he wanted to wear black trousers, white shirt and black bow tie to the school Christmas dance. Remembering my failure to interest his older brothers in kilts, jackets, ties of all sort for their school dances, I couldn't account for this. Until I went to collect him. All the Chinese and Pakistani boys were dressed as waiters. Of course they were. They *are*, at weekends.

A WEE DOMESTIC CRISIS

James Pagan

ON THE 18TH November 1795 the Clyde again "wide o'er the brim with many a torrent swelled"; and as before, the lower parts of the city were completely submerged. About midday two of the arches of the bridge, then recently erected at the foot of Saltmarket, fell down with a crash, and the displacement of water was so tremendous that the doors of the public washing-houses, though situated at a great distance, were burst open, and a portion of the clothes and utensils floated away. The remaining arches fell in the course of the afternoon, and thus the edifice was entirely destroyed. During this flood a boy was drowned in attempting to reach his home at the foot of the New Wynd.

Amidst all these distressing occurrences there happened one so comic that its recital by the tittle-tattlers of the day made people almost forget the general calamity caused by the flood. It seemed that David Dale, Esq., whose house was situated at the foot of Charlotte Street, had invited a large party to dinner on the said 18th day of November 1795, and expected William Simpson, cashier at the Royal Bank; the great millionaire, Gilbert Innes of Stowe; and the whole posse of the Royal Bank directory, to come from Edinburgh to meet George Moncrieff, George McIntosh, and a few other Glasgow magnates at dinner on the said day.

On the memorable morning of the said 18th all was bustle and hurry-burry in Mr Dale's house, preparing a sumptuous feast for this distinguished party. The kitchen fires were in full blaze, prompt to roast the jolly joints of meat already skewered on the spits, to boil the well-stuffed turkeys, and to stew the other tit-bits of the table; while the puddings and custards stood ready on the dresser for immediate application to the bars of the grate; when, lo and behold! the waters of the Clyde began gently to ooze through the chinks of the kitchen floor, and by-and-by gradually to increase, so that in a short time the servants came to be going about their work with the water above their ankles.

At this critical moment the Monkland Canal burst its banks, and, like an avalanche, the water came thundering down the Molendinar Burn, carrying all before it, and filling the low houses of the Gallowgate, Saltmarket, Bridgegate, and under portions of St Andrew's Square with a muddy stream, and the wrecks of many a poor man's dwelling.

In consequence of the regorgement of water caused by the said mishap, and the continued increase of the flood, the Camlachie Burn, which ran close by Mr Dale's house, was raised to an unusual height, and at once with a crash, broke into Mr Dale's kitchen, putting out all the fires there, and making the servants run for their lives, they having scarcely had time to save the half-dressed dinner.

Then came the great question, what was now to be done? The dinner hour was fast approaching, and the great Edinburgh visitors were already whirling rapidly towards Glasgow in their carriages; while the fires of the kitchen being completely extinguished, the kitchen itself was thereby rendered totally useless. In this calamitous dilemma, Mr Dale applied to his opposite neighbour in Charlotte Street, Mr William Wardlaw, for the loan of his kitchen; and also to another of his neighbours, Mr Archibald Paterson, for a like accommodation; both of whom not only readily granted the use of their kitchens but also the aid of their servants to cook Mr Dale's dinner.

But still the question remained, how were the wines, spirits, and ales to be gotten from the cellar which now stood four feet deep in water? After much cogitation, a porter was hired, who, being suitably dressed for the occasion, was to descend to the abyss and bring up the said articles. It, however, occurred to Mr Dale that the porter would not be able to distinguish the bins that contained the port, sherry, and Madeira (Mr Dale did not sport French wines) from those of the rum, brandy, porter and ale.

In this emergency, Miss Dale, then sixteen years of age, was mounted on the porter's back, and both having descended to the cellar, Miss Dale, amidst the waters of the deep, pointed out to her chevalier where he was to find the different articles for the table. After having received instructions the porter brought up his fair charge to the lobby of the house, where Miss Dale dismounted from the shoulders of her bearer in safety; and the porter having again descended to the cellar, readily found the wines and ales that were wanted, which he delivered to Mr Dale in good order.

All things now went on in a satisfactory manner. The Edinburgh visitors and Glasgow magnates arrived in due time, the dinner was cooked and placed on the table in the best of style, and the whole party passed the evening in mirth and jocularity at the odd circumstances which had attended this merry meeting.

Glasgow Past and Present

GORBALS: A LOST HORIZON

John Burrowes

THERE ARE CERTAIN sights in this world, very special, very personal, which jolt the system so much that the mind freezes the scene forever; a mental video that can be everlastingly re-run with all the accompanying sensations of real life. We all have them, in varying numbers, varying kinds. Maybe you're a traveller, someone who has been to far-off places, places even further than Benidorm, and there'll be some exotic sights in your collection. Some are more personal . . . a wedding, a birth. Some traumatic . . . a war, an accident. Some sensational . . . winning a title, an award, maybe even a fortune. Some are a mixture of all the categories. I have my own collection and one of the earliest is one of the jewels. It sounds more like the title for a school essay than the memory of a lifetime. Quite simply it is . . . the first impression of Florence Street.

Florence Street was in the Gorbals. My childhood life was spent in the neighbouring suburb of Govanhill. By comparison to the Gorbals, Govanhill was what you might call . . . sedate. Well, for a start, Gorbals had 118 pubs. Govanhill had none. Its population density was only a fraction of its gutsy boundary mate and there were other advantages, none of which were appreciated by young children, except, of course, that the Malls Myre was nearer and the Malls Myre was Adventure—with slagheaps, hillocks and a big slimy pond that had frogs in the spring. All my family came from the Gorbals and we would return there weekly for that passing custom, the Sunday visit. The first visit I can remember, the one which was to be forever remembered, occurred some time in the mid-thirties. I was about seven years of age, perhaps younger.

It was a simple walk from Govanhill to the Gorbals . . . into Cathcart Road, cobbled and tram-lined, and head north along what was at the time one of the finest shopping thoroughfares in the south side; Italian warehousemen and fruitshops that cooked their own beets in cellars beneath pavement grilles; furniture stores and grain stores; fishmongers and ironmongers; confectioners and cafés (and who could make better fish suppers than Giusti's?); linoleum shops and wool shops; even an egg shop. There was a wooden dance hall called the Lido which looked like a coffin with doors, and churches with great names like the Candlish Memorial where my sister used to take me to the Band of Hope for the songs and the tea-and-bun supper.

Govanhill came to an end after Aikenhead Road, at the point where Cathcart Road crossed the long bridge over the London Midland and Scottish railway tracks, six of them, or was it eight? From there, at almost every minute of the day, you could see a train of sorts: ones pulling trucks to the Gushetfaulds Goods Yards; squat puggy engines on the Govan Colliery line; shunting engines bullying long lines of waggons; and if you saw an extra-long passenger train with a really big engine, the kind that had three giant wheels on either side, then that was the London train; so they said anyway.

After the bridge there was a kind of no man's land of waste ground, a lane that led to a row of miners' red-brick cottages called the Lower English Buildings and then past the billboards with the sailor and his Player's cigarettes and the toucan and its Guinness, down the gentle descent to the junction they called the Gushet where the white tram took the right fork, the red tram the left one. Then you reached Dixon's Blazes, the ironworks. The spewing and belching of steam and smoke, the hideous smells and thundering screams and dins from steam valves and giant hammers made you think it was Hell itself that was happening behind its high walls and you quickened your pace lest some evil hand was to reach out for you.

Thereafter you were in Crown Street, one of the principal arteries of the Gorbals, busier even than Cathcart Road and where the Gorbals man, or woman, could get every requisite in life, not least the enjoyment of the pub.

Of course, you don't know about pubs when you're a child of six or seven, but Crown Street had them just the same. There was The Tap, Milligan's (Tommy Milligan's no less, he that fought Mickey Walker for the middleweight champion-ship of the world), the Waverley and Teacher's, Souter's and Archibald's, Urquhart's and the Wee Man's, The Wheatsheaf, Jackson's and The Lion, The Grapes, Hurrell's and the Moulin Rouge. Maybe there were others!

Crown Street! It seemed like a whole town by itself. A community with tram-lines up the middle. A place to live; a place for living. Florence Street was one street parallel to the east from Crown Street and, if it was the top end you wanted, you could get to it from Crown Street by turning right at Kames Street—smallest street in the Gorbals, or so it appeared—Kidston Street, Caledonia Road or Cumberland Street. We turned at the latter, distinguished by one of Sillitoe's police boxes and the railings round the stairs which led to the underground lavatories.

I had no idea, really, what to expect on that day when my mind had matured sufficiently to have memory capability. We reached the corner with the licensed grocer called Crosgroves at one end and a public house called The Moy at the other. And, behold . . . there was Florence Street.

Something very magic, very special happened at the sight of what lay before me. It was like what befell Ronald Colman, Edward Everett Horton and the party after their plane had crashed in the Tibetan wastes in the old film classic of *Lost Horizon*.

There they were, stranded in the wind and sleet and bitter cold and the character called Mallinson declares, "Good God, Conway! What sort of Hell's kitchen are we making for?" Then, suddenly, the ground levelled and the party stepped out of the mist into clear sunny air and what they saw was "indeed a strange and almost incredible sight . . . a deep sensation, half mystical, half visual, of having reached some place that was an end . . . a finality".

Florence Street was indeed a strange and incredible sight for a seven-year-old who had seen nothing like it before. For it seemed like the world's biggest and busiest playground. And it was packed with the greatest number of children I had ever seen together in one place. Thousands of them. Weans of every conceivable description . . . Proddie weans, Pape weans, Parish weans—they were the ones with the good boots and the long socks with red and black stripes—pimpled weans, snott'ry-nosed weans, fighting weans, happy weans, greetin' weans, throw-me-doon-a-piece-Maw weans, weans playing at beds, at rounders, at football, at actors and actresses (a step for a point and see who gets across the road first), at dodgie ball and tig; wee lassies in groups playing schools or hospitals, boys in other groups with their home-made equipment, barrows and bogeys, scooters and . . . don't let anybody kid you skateboards are a recent invention. They had home-made skateboards as well.

That first sighting on that particular day is the deepest-etched memory of any single event in my mind and irrespective of what that might indicate, I had found my Lost Horizon. The house at number 188, where my grandparents and aunts and uncles and cousins lived, two closes from the Moy, was to be my Shangri-La and my cousin John, about the same age as myself, was the Dalai Lama.

And everything about Florence Street remained that way for the ensuing years of childhood. I learned my streetcraft there: to be first off your mark if the Busies came and you were playing football; and to be just as quick when the bad boys from round in Camden Street came looking for trouble.

Alas, nothing is permanent. The acquisition of adolescence then adulthood—the getting of Wisdom!—saw Florence Street and the Gorbals in another light. Six years of war and neglect had left it in a mess and when some landlords realised how much it would cost to restore their ageing tenements to such basic standards as

No, not that miracle, another one

The Gorbals, pre-Spence

being wind and watertight, they fled. Their ship was sinking. Some formed limited companies so that when their properties were no longer profitable and the authorities insisted that they must be repaired they could glibly declare they were "out of funds". Others, in order to avoid repairs or, worse still, being forced to pay for the demolition of buildings declared structurally dangerous, "sold" them off to worthless men for even less than thirty pieces, thus leaving the burden on the council. The ruse was that if the council pursued the penniless new owners for liabilities they would get nothing. Even the law accepts that you can't take blood from a stone.

And there were other manoeuvres to avoid their moral duties. The landlords retreated in their droves, finding new outlets for the capital with which they had milked the Gorbals for decades. They lived in some surprising places . . . like Surrey and Sussex, mock people in mock Tudors; France and Sweden; c/o the India Club in London; the New Town in Edinburgh; the big stone villas of Perth and Dumfries and Aberdeen and, in the case of my relatives' house at number 188 Florence Street, the other eleven houses up the close and all those in two neighbouring closes and two shops, the owners were a minister and his wife from Craigellachie in Inverness-shire. Imagine my Shangri-La being owned by a man of the cloth! And him no' even a lama! No wonder Burns said you had to beware of the Black Craws.

The landlords raped Florence Street—then they cast her aside with as much respect as they would for some old whore. They did the same for Old Florence's friends, the other streets of the Gorbals. Raped and abandoned, the district was left to the mercy of the local authority, at that time the Glasgow Corporation. To some this may have seemed like Dracula handing over to Frankenstein. Sadly, it was to be a fair analogy, the way things were to eventuate, for if one had been a bloodsucker, the other was to be a monster. One ravished; the other was to ravage.

In 1965, twenty years after the end of the war, Christian Action was so moved by the pitiful state of the district that it asked the Press to meet for a special pronouncement on the area. I was there at St Paul's when the great church's Canon and Treasurer, the late Canon John Collins, then president of Christian Action, delivered the findings of his organisation. The document which they had prepared was aptly titled . . . *A Mean City*. It contained some fearsome facts:

* 63 per cent of the houses in the heart of the Gorbals were insanitary and structurally unfit.
* 99 per cent of the buildings were of the lowest structural category.
* The landlords had a total ignorance of the law as it related to their duties.
* The landlords were in the main negligent . . . and many were making profits of several hundred per cent per week.

Surrounded by hostile forces

Predictably, the kind of people who never seem to be in short supply in Glasgow City Chambers threw up their arms in disbelief at what they termed as a slur on them. Said one councillor, "It's not true. I think there's been a miracle in the Gorbals." Said another, the Senior Magistrate, "No one can accuse us of not taking any action." And the local Member of Parliament, a former councillor, hit out with, "To say we are the worst in Europe is nonsense."

The transparency of politicians! You can almost read their how-much-is-the-dogma-in-the-window signs. And if the signs had an answer it would be . . . "votes".

Eventually however, Glasgow Corporation put its Gorbals redevelopment plan into full operation. This was done in such a fashion that it appeared that someone was out for revenge; as though they wanted to obliterate every single aspect of the form and shape and character of the once colourful community; as though they wanted to show the world that when they finished there wouldn't be a single trace of *No Mean City* about the place.

And, to that end, they were highly successful. They tore out its heart of flesh and gave it one of concrete. Old Rutherglen Road got award-winning multi-storey flats designed by Sir Basil Spence, no less; they've got all the grace of the old Maryhill Barracks on stilts. The Oatlands end of Caledonia Road and around Adelphi Street got the customary off-the-peg multi—vertical streets where the electric lifts lead to loneliness and which inspire either Valium or psychosis or both. At the Gorbals Cross and western end of the suburb they boxed them up in other versions of perpendicular people farms. And around Florence Street, in the old heartland of the district, they were given what was said to be a showpiece garden development . . . designed and landscaped so that the old outline of the street was no longer recognisable.

On this site they erected twelve seven-storey blocks of flats—with all the style and elegance of giant bus shelters. Seven hundred and fifty-six families had untold misery heaped on them as a result of being allocated these houses, which, it turned out, were hopelessly inadequate for the rigours of the Scottish climate. Fungus

They made a desert, and called it urbanology

grew from bedroom walls, clothes disintegrated in wardrobes, wallpaper peeled, and carpets furred with white mould. Those living in the houses most afflicted with damp were, over the years, rehoused—leaving behind families miserably isolated amidst empty houses and at the mercy of all sorts of miscreants. They endured such a hellish existence thereafter that they too had to be evacuated and given other houses.

Ten years after they were opened, every one of them had been vacated. They now stand sodden and vandalised as a grotesque monument to all that is bad about Glasgow's administration. The good people of the Gorbals never deserved the landlords who took their fill and ran away. Nor did they deserve the kind of people who keep telling us Glasgow is miles better—and made places like the Gorbals miles worse. Some of them expected accolades for what they did to the Gorbals. They get none from me . . . for they made a Lost Horizon lost forever.

THE BALLAD OF MUCKY FU

William McIlvanney

His alias is Jimmy. If you see him oan the street,
He'll likely have the wife wi' him an' weans aboot his feet.
He'll be noddin' like, or laughin' an' actin' kinna saft.
He might look an easy contract but the wee print's "Don't be daft".

There's a magic amber liquid that he swallies every night.
Each gless contains a cubit that is added tae his height.
Jist watch the transformation. He becomes, efter a few,
A tartan belt in martial arts, the dreaded Mucky Fu.

He'll mutter mystic formulae like some wild, ancient sage
In a language never written but passed doon fae rage tae rage.
"Ya bam, ya get, ye're gonny, right, that's it, nae chance, okay,
Moothfu' o' heiders, dull yin, name yer next o'kin," he'll say,

"Play keepie-uppie wi' ye, make a jigsaw o' yer face,
Open a windae wi' yer heid an' ventilate the place,
Show ye hoo tae eat yer teeth if you don't show respect,
A jeely-jaur'll haud whit's left" — or words to that effect.

Big polismen are always turnin' up whaur he has been
An', awestruck, they survey the devastation o' the scene.
But only raw recruits think they are seein' somethin' new.
The constable says, "Atom bomb?" The sergeant, "Mucky Fu".

He wid make a boay o' Superman, a monkey o' King Kong.
He has lit his fag at Etna, he has heard the sirens' song.
He telt them they were rubbish, they'd be better oan the broo.
As they killed themselves their last wail wis an eerie "Mucky Fu".

You will find him in the outback, you will see him in Bahrain,
He has roamed the Altiplano an' the middle western plain.
An' in Samarkand an' Delhi an' Hong Kong an' Timbuktu
Many natives fled in panic, quaintly screamin' "Mucka Fu".

If ye take a wee refreshment an' a wee Glaswegian's there,
Keep a close watch oan him but be careful no' tae stare.
As the amber liquid vanishes, hum, "Nearer, God, tae you."
An' be shair that you're polite tae him. He might be Mucky Fu.

The grape that doth with Logic absolute
The seven and seventy jarring sects confute . . .

City of dreaming spires

PRETTY TOWN

Tobias Smollett

I AM SO far happy to have seen Glasgow, which, to the best of my recollection and judgment, is one of the prettiest towns in Europe; and without all doubt, it is one of the most flourishing in Great Britain. It stands partly on a gentle declivity; but the greatest part of it is a plain, watered by the river Clyde. The streets are straight, open, airy and well paved; and the houses lofty and well built, of hewn stone. At the upper end of the town, there is a venerable cathedral, that may be compared with York-minster or Westminster; and, about the middle of the descent from this to the Cross, is the College, a respectable pile of building, with all manner of accommodation for the professors and students, including an excellent library, and an observatory well provided with astronomical instruments. The number of inhabitants is said to amount to thirty thousand; and marks of opulence and independency appear in every quarter of this commercial city, which, however, is not without its inconveniences and defects. The water of their public pumps is generally hard and brackish, an imperfection of the less excusable, as the river Clyde runs by their doors, in the lower part of the town; and there are rivulets and springs above the cathedral, sufficient to fill a large reservoir with excellent water, which might thence be distributed to all the different parts of the city. It is of more consequence to consult the health of the inhabitants in this article than to employ so much attention in beautifying their town with new streets, squares and churches.

Another defect, not easily remedied, is the shallowness of the river, which will not float vessels of any burden within ten or twelve miles of the city; so that the merchants are obliged to load and unload their ships at Greenock and Port-Glasgow, situated about fourteen miles nearer the mouth of the firth, where it is about two miles broad. The people of Glasgow have a noble spirit of enterprise.

The Expedition of Humphry Clinker

INFINITE VARIETY

Chris Young

I LIKE GLASGOW. I really do like the place. Although I was born in Scotland's capital, I have spent the greater part of my adult life in or near the city of Glasgow, and I feel more at home here than anywhere else. It is my happy task to write a few pages on the history of the Glasgow Variety theatres that were so much a part of the lives of the good citizens of the Green Place in days gone by. It is a labour of love.

Arguably, the Glasgow Empire was the most famous Variety Theatre in Great Britain, with the possible exception of the London Palladium. So let us begin our story there.

Legends were made at the Empire. Some of the real legends of world show-business graced its boards: Sinatra; Garland; Martin and Lewis; Laurel and Hardy; Danny Kaye; Bob Hope. Yes, they were all Americans. But our lot were also well represented: Morecambe and Wise; Tommy Cooper; Bruce Forsyth . . . oh, stop namedropping . . . we all know that the Empire booked the best. But the theatre also saw the very worst of its star-studded variety bills. It had a name as being a graveyard for English comedians, and I wondered why. I thought it might have been an accent thing. You know what I mean? In the days before most homes had television sets that somehow educated us not only to recognise but also to understand the Cockney or, say, the Scouse accent, it must have been very difficult for an English comedian to make himself understood in Scotland. Even our own great comedian of the interwar years—Tommy Lorne—was thought at first to be a risky bet when he starred in pantomime for the first time in Edinburgh, so thick was his Glasgow accent. The only reason the promoters took a chance was that he was a great visual comic and he needed few words.

But you do see what I mean? The distance of even forty-odd miles between Glasgow and Edinburgh could make all the difference.

Let's start back to front if you like. The Russians closed the place. It's true. The last attraction at the Glasgow Empire before it closed its doors for the last time in March 1963 was the Red Army Ensemble. Now let me tell you how it all began.

The site of the Glasgow Empire was once the Old Choral Hall. In 1894 it was converted and opened as a Music Hall called The Gaiety by a fellow called D. S. Mackay. He also managed what were known as "Penny Geggies" in his native Dundee. Penny Geggies were small theatres of the type that were beginning to spring up in every town in Scotland as the Music Hall gained in popularity.

Mackay did not do very well, so the following year he sold the theatre to one Charles Bernard who ran it as a Musical Playhouse. Two years later it closed, having been acquired by H. E. Moss and James Kirk, who opened the much larger Empire Palace Theatre, built on the same site in 1897. The name Moss will go down in the history books because he and his partners founded the most prestigious chain of variety theatres in Britain, and for many years Europe, Moss Empires.

The Empire closed again in August 1930 for major alterations; it was enlarged and reopened in September 1931. From that time it was to become known as "The Home of The Stars" and the short list of international showbusiness luminaries at the beginning of this chapter will tell you why.

Essential frivolity

It was a visit to the Empire that persuaded the young Harry Lauder to try his luck in London. He might well have settled for a career trudging around the halls in Scotland had he not gone one night to see the great Dan Leno at work in the Empire. Lauder was informed that Dan Leno was being paid a hundred pounds for his week's stint at the Glasgow Empire. It was enough to persuade him to go South in search of stardom. He reasoned that although he might make a fairly good living in Scotland, he could do rather better should he find success in London. Then he could come home a star and command a much larger salary. It is enough to say that is exactly what happened.

In 1953 when Frank Sinatra played the Empire, his star was in the descendant. Sinatra had been the biggest name in showbusiness in the post-war period. But his record sales and movie career had slipped. The fans had deserted him, and when he came to town he played to poor audiences for his week at the Empire. That's show-business. Yet it was when he was in Glasgow that Sinatra's manager, Hank Sanicola, received a telegram from Hollywood to tell him that his boy had won the Critics' Award for his performance as Private Maggio in the film *From Here To Eternity*. A couple of months later Sinatra also won the Oscar for the same performance, and he was once again back on top.

Talk about a turning point. Judy Garland had a similar experience. She had come to Britain to play the London Palladium in 1951 just after she had been dropped by MGM. The Hollywood moguls thought she was all washed up, but after a hugely successful tour of Britain which included weeks at both the Glasgow and Edinburgh Empires, she returned to America with renewed confidence, and took on the mighty Palace Theatre in New York. She played there for twenty-seven consecutive weeks, and was back in the big-time once again with Hollywood producers lining up to get her signature on a contract.

I mentioned that great theatrical family Moss. When they opened the Glasgow Empire in 1897, that event led to the closure of another Glasgow theatre that the family owned: the Scotia down on Stockwell Street.

To tell something of the story of the Scotia we have to go back in time a very long way indeed—the very beginnings of Music Hall in Scotland. The Scotia was, indeed is, a public house. As long ago as 1830 it offered entertainment of the free-and-easy type. Many pubs in Glasgow had this type of entertainment in those days. There was for example the Philharmonic in Dunlop Street, the Shakespeare and the Jupiter, both in the Saltmarket area, the Whitebait in St Enoch's Wynd, and Campbell's in the Trongate. All had little shows and all vied to attract the customers. Occasionally a strolling player would be paid to entertain, but most of the time the customers themselves were encouraged to perform for the odd free drink, or a penny or two if they proved really popular with the clientèle.

The Scotia had been a public house for many years before a fellow by the name of James Bayliss came along and bought the place with the view to building a Music Hall on to the premises. Bayliss had once been the chairman at the Oddfellows Music Hall in Glasgow, but had left that place in something of a hurry. One evening, whilst our James was doing his Leonard Sachs bit, a drunk in the audience who did not care for his patter threw a bottle at him and the unfortunate Bayliss

Jimmy Logan

lost an eye. Swift exit. He then went into business for himself, opening two Music Halls in the Cowcaddens area before moving on to Stockwell Street and the Scotia.

Bayliss and succeeding managements at the theatre turned the place into one of the most famous little theatres in Britain. Following Bayliss came H. E. Moss, son of James Moss, the founder of that Empire chain of halls. Under that banner many luminaries of the Music Hall graced the boards at the theatre, including Vesta Tilley and a very young Henry MacLellan Lauder, later Sir Harry and the first knight of the Music Hall, who played one of his very first professional engagements at the Scotia.

Moss closed the Scotia in 1897 when he opened the Empire Theatre, but it reopened the following year under new management. Then, in 1901, and having been renamed the Metropole, it was taken over by Arthur Jefferson.

Arthur Jefferson had been a successful comedian in his time, and made an extremely good living on the halls in the North of England. As impresario he developed a little chain of theatres which stretched from North Shields to Motherwell. Very laudable. But more important, he was the father of one of the most famous film comedians of our times, Stan Laurel.

Stan was a teenager when he came to Glasgow with his parents and finished his education here at schools both in Rutherglen and Queen's Park. He also got his first taste of showbusiness in the city when he entered a "Go As You Please" competition at the Panopticon Theatre in Argyle Street. Incidentally, that little hall can still be seen today, if one should take the trouble to find a certain shoe shop on Argyle Street and speak kindly to the manager of the premises. Above the shop are store rooms, and those store rooms have been left really as they were when the place was a theatre. Through the cobwebs one can see the old proscenium arch of the Panopticon. I went there recently, and had the strangest feeling as I stood there, knowing the stories about the place. Laurel aside, one of our own most famous entertainers, Jack Buchanan, took his first faltering steps in the ranks of the professional entertainers in that theatre. Ghosts.

Back to the Metropole. In 1943 a man called Jack Short took charge of production there under the management of the family Frutin who had taken over round about the time of the First World War. Jack and his missus, May Dalziel, formed a family show there in 1947. It was called The Logan Family, and it was to become an institution at the Metropole. Jack's son, Jimmy Logan, who took his stage name from his aunt, Ella Logan, a Broadway and Hollywood star, became a star in his own right at the Met when he was all of sixteen-years-old.

Like many another great little theatre, the Met was destroyed by fire. It happened on 28 October 1961. So many new talents emerged from the Met that it would be impossible to list them all, but one I must mention is Tommy Morgan.

Tommy was a big moon-faced Clydesider from Brigton, I do beg your pardon, I mean Bridgeton. He was a Glasgow comic loved by his public and fellow professionals alike, and he played in many pantos at the Met before moving to the next theatre I want to tell you about. The Pavilion. Tommy Morgan made the Pavilion Theatre his summer residence for a score of years, and he packed them into the Renfield Street theatre in their thousands. An Honest Chiel. A very funny man. Even today, almost thirty years after his death, his name is remembered fondly by everyone who knew him.

The Pavilion itself opened in 1904, and was regarded at the time as the last thing in luxury, a modern theatre with all the trappings of a plush West End hall. From the beginning the management's policy was to book only the very best, and for years it was rated as the most successful theatre in Glasgow if not in Scotland.

Even with the mighty Glasgow Empire as its neighbour, the Pavilion flourished. It was not uncommon for theatre-goers to make the first house of the Empire then cross the street to catch the second performance at the Pavilion. Tommy Morgan himself was asked if he feared the competition from the Empire when he was in summer season at Renfield Street. Tommy wasn't worried. "Naw. They'll still come tae see me. Ye cannae go and see Danny Kaye every night o' the week." It made sense.

The palmy days at the Pavilion really ended with the late great Lex McLean. Like Morgan before him, Lex was an institution at that theatre. Rain, hail or snow, they flocked to see him. He was quite simply a great show. People left feeling so much better than when they had arrived. McLean was a tonic.

Of course the Pavilion always did have a great tradition for comedy, and all our superb Scots comedians played the theatre at one time or another. Will Fyfe was a struggling young character actor turned variety comic when he first introduced his famous "I Belong to Glasgow" in his act at the Pavilion. In the best theatrical traditions he was "discovered" and the rest, as they say, is showbiz history. Jack

Anthony found it "nae bother at a'" to get laughs at the Pavilion, and in the years between the wars Tommy Lorne was box-office magic.

I have probably hurt some feelings by not mentioning so many other entertainers in this chapter, but really that was not the purpose of the exercise. This is just a brief look back at an age now gone forever, but still lamented—and cherished. A magic age.

It'll be all right on the night

CUE FOR A SONG

Norman White

I FIRST CAME to Glasgow in 1967, from Cheshire, to rehearse with Scottish Opera for the Edinburgh Festival. The buildings were black and gloomy, unlike today's glorious revelations, and perhaps it was the wettest summer of all time. The weather might have been designed to clean the place. It rained for seven weeks.

Rehearsals were in a broken-down warehouse in Stobcross Street, just about where the Kingston Bridge is now, and I remember it for all the buckets spread around to collect rain through the roof. All the fabulous music of Haydn, Bellini and Stravinsky played to the accompaniment of raindrops, like dozens of metronomes running at different speeds. And picking my way over the forms of unconscious drunks in the morning, left over from the night before.

Happily all the gloom of the weather was washed away by the warmth of the Glaswegians. Like other strangers I wondered who Jimmy was till I discovered it was me. And I learned that Glasgow was the only city in the world where first

The natives are friendly

Artist at work

thing in the morning you could throw open the curtains and then the windows and listen to the birds coughing.

Some people take opera rather solemnly. It isn't solemn from inside. I remember the dress rehearsal of our lavish production of *The Trojans* (all six hours of it), when the spectacular wooden horse was pushed on-stage, full of extras. Unfortunately, instead of moving to centre stage it went through the floor. At an actual performance one of the extras was afraid to jump out of the horse, so he was pushed. He suffered a broken arm and a lot of embarrassment. Imagine arriving at the hospital, being asked how it happened, and having to say, "I fell out of a horse".

At another performance, Wagner's mighty *Rheingold,* all seriousness was lost when Bill McCue's staff went straight throught the stage. He was one of the two giants who have built Valhalla and have to be paid in gold to hide the goddess standing behind; the gold is stacked against their staffs, which are rammed into the ground. The clip that should have held Bill's staff was non-functioning. Suddenly there was no singing, only the heaving of his shoulders as he yanked it out, dropped it in again and was left with about a foot of it showing.

"For Christ's stake," he muttered to the goddess, "kneel!"

The real thrill throughout that time, however, was the opera-starved audiences on their feet shouting for more.

Outside of the opera, I lived by exploration. The red trains on the Underground were so small I couldn't believe people could actually get into them. And since I was on tour so much, I couldn't get used to the tiny beds in Scottish digs. I later discovered that the standard Scottish mattress, designed to fit into hole-in-the-wall beds, was four feet eight; and I thought this might have some mystic connection with sleepers, since the guage of railway tracks is just about the same. Another great find was the pedestrian tunnels under the Clyde, exits and entrances guarded by Glasgow pigeons. Nobody seemed to know they were there.

But it's the people. It would be impossible to be lonely here. Go into any pub and within minutes you can make new friends and have long discussions on any subject you like. Glasgow is arguably the best arguable town in the world.

FUNNY?

D. Macleod Malloch

THE CITIZEN of Glasgow is not, generally speaking, a very witty person, but he possesses in some degree that dry humour which is to be found in most Scotsmen. Everyone is aware that all Englishmen believe, or at least say, that Scotsmen are devoid of humour and are unable to see a joke; but recently one writer has been found courageous enough to assert that all the inhabitants of Scotland are humorous.

This seems a fairly strong claim; but it is not very wide of the mark so far as dry and caustic humour is concerned. The shallow wit which appeals to the average Londoner is conspicuously absent in Glasgow. But despite an unfavourable climate and a smoke-laden atmosphere, the Glasgow Scot occasionally managed to make a joke, even if it is made "wi' deeficulty". In the following anecdotes the idea has been to illustrate the types of humour which are perhaps most frequently to be found in Glasgow, and, generally speaking, the dry and caustic is principally in evidence.

The following story exhibits both traditional Scottish canniness and dry sarcasm:

A somewhat parsimonious couple invited a friend to dine with them on a Monday, and when the joint was laid on the table it proved to be the remains of Sunday's roast heated up. Whereupon the guest remarked that this appeared to be "an auld frien' with a new face". This, however, did not prevent his doing justice to the fare provided; and upon departing he said, "Well, good night. I've had an enjoyable evening; and you have always the consolation that it hasna cost you too much."

The Book of Glasgow Anecdote

A FAREWELL TO GLASGOW

Carl MacDougall

JESUS CHRIST, eh. It's a great game played slow but intit. How you doing pal? You okay? That's good; so am I.

You a student? You look like a student. You a teacher? Look, if I'm being too cheeky just tell us to shut up or something. I'm just talking. It's nice to be nice but intit. You in the town?

I'll give you it for a tanner, cash

Aye. I came in to pay the union; it was that warm a couple of us went for a wee pint then you know yourself the usual happened, session; skoosh cash with they dominoes but. Never mind. I'm off for a wee kip, then I'll take her out and keep her mouth shut.

See this bus, pure rubbish, so it is but. Look at that. That's they weans. Pure vandals. See up our way, you cannae get a phone nor nothing, neer ye kin but. Bloody liberty. I mean, see this place man, it's finished. No that it ever was up to much; it was aye Glesca and anythin'll do them.

If you ask me, it's the Government's fault. I mean, you take they Tories shouting and bawling about the state of the country. What do they know about it; half of them don't even live here. See that Mrs Thatcher, her maw used to keep a wee rag store ower on the sooth side. Scandal, so it is. If you ask me, the Tories get as much as they kin while they're in, then they let the Labour in to clear up the mess. See, they Labour clowns gie ye a load of fanny about helping everybody and all the time they're helping themselves.

Look at this ile. I mean, what are the Yanks doing here. Not that long ago you never saw a Yank here unless he was lost. You'd've needed to start a war to get them over and even then they wouldnae've come. They'd've sent big John Wayne over and he'd've won it for them. They're here for what they can get. And they're getting plenty, cause if they werenae they widnae be here. If they could sook as hard as they kin blaw they'd have all that ile over there nae bother, and aa the whales and fishes along with it.

I don't know. I'm fed up. See that SNP, they're the same as the Yanks, in it for number one. They're worse. They'll tell you anything to get in. They'd a fellow on

Intermission

the other night, know what he said? Listen to this. We'll aa get cheaper fish suppers once they're in. What do you think of that, eh? It's a fact. Cheaper fish suppers. I think they think our heids button up the back or something. Then he said we were all going to get cheaper whisky. Fucksake. A hauf's going to cost hauf of what it does now. O. Soon as he said that, all the clowns in the pub are cheering, Hullooo. I don't know, they'd tell you anything to get in, anything at all. Crowd of chancers the whole bloody lot of them.

Telling you man, this place is finished. I'm getting right out of this dump; going up north, up to where the money is, on they rigs or something. They've got camps with wee challeys aa to yourself, naebody to bother you and the best of gear. Pubs with groups singing and that. Seen it on the telly. Five hundred quid a week they're getting. Fucksake, Sinatra doesnae get that for a week at the Caesar's Palace. Five hundred notes slapped right in your paw. I've got a big mate up there and he'll get us a start. I mean, how could you get money like that in this dump; couldnae, could ye. You've got to work for it. Don't know what the work's like, but it's work intit. What's any work like.

Is this your stop? You going? Aye, well, see you again, eh. Mind and keep a look out for they flying coos. See ye, pal.

DISASTER

Andrew McQueen

THE LAST accident of this kind on the river took place at the Broomielaw on 5th February 1851, two deaths resulting. A handsome little two-funnelled steamer called the *Plover*, reckoned to be the fastest on the river, was lying at her berth that morning, due to start at half-past seven for Bowling, in connection with the Dunbartonshire Railway. She had been built by Messrs Wingate about two years before, and her steeple-engine of about 80 horsepower, together with her two haystack boilers, had been constructed from the designs of David Napier.

Suddenly, a little after seven o'clock, a loud report echoed over a large portion of the city, and the dwellers in Carlton Place awoke from their slumbers and rubbed their sleepy eyes in alarm, wondering if a dreadful thunderbolt had expended itself over the city. The after-boiler of the *Plover* had exploded, killing the engineer and terribly scalding two firemen, one of whom succumbed a day or two later in the infirmary. The force of the explosion was such that a piece of the outer covering of the boiler, measuring about 60 square feet, swept along the after-deck, clearing away everything in its path, including the companion and the funnel of the cabin stove, while a piece of metal weighing about quarter of a hundredweight was blown clean over some high houses on the north side of the river and fell in Ann Street, a hundred yards away.

The dome of the boiler was blown to pieces, the funnel falling over the starboard side into the river and smashing the paddle-box in its descent. The steamer, in common with the other boats of the period, had no proper bridge, but simply a sort of gangway between the paddle-boxes, on which the steering-wheel was placed. This was smashed to pieces by the explosion and the wheel destroyed.

It appears that the after-boiler had been emptied the previous evening, to receive some repairs, and after these had been effected water had been injected by means of a hand pump. It is conjectured that the quantity thus put in had been insufficient to cover the top of the firebox and tube-plate, which had consequently become red-hot, and that as soon as the donkey-engine was set to work to pump more water into the boiler, steam had been generated so rapidly and in such volume that the safety-valves, of which there were two, were quite inadequate to give it egress, and the boiler itself had to give way.

It would not have been surprising if this accident had had an injurious effect on the Broomielaw steamboat trade, or even if something of a panic had ensued, but no such untoward consequences occurred. The Glasgow citizen of the period was too fond of his sail "doon the watter" to be deterred from it by anything so unlikely as a boiler explosion; so much so that on the Spring Fast-Day, just two months after the mishap, the majority of the twenty-three steamers that sailed on excursions from the Broomielaw had to put off from the wharf, completely filled, before the advertised hour of sailing.

Nor does any apprehension appear to have been allowed to mar the joys of the day's outing, as we learn from a contemporary scribe that before Glasgow was reached on the return journey "many of the male passengers had become intoxicated", and that "only the strenuous exertions of police-officers and assistant harbourmasters prevented a serious loss of life, for these not only prevented some people from falling into the river, but pulled others out after they had got in". Evidently, to anyone who took his holiday in such thorough fashion, the possible bursting of a boiler was but a minor risk.

Echoes of Old Clyde Paddle-Wheels

AH'M SPLITTIN'

Agnes McLean

TO BREAK INTO the big-time social scene in Glasgow in the Thirties one had to be a rerr dancer. There were literally hundreds of dance halls in Glasgow, from the classy Plaza and Albert to the not-so-classy Hibs, Tower, and Tripe (the Tripe was an empty shop in the Tradeston area, with the band stuck up on a shelf in a corner).

How then did one reach the exalted position of being a rerr dancer? I was lucky. My pal had five brothers, four of whom were keen ballroom dancers. Every other night they practised dancing up and down the close with my pal and me as their partners.

The close played a very important social role in the community. The close was where all the tenants met to solve the tenement's problems. The close was where we children played and held concerts. The close was a dance floor. The close was where romances started, developed and matured. The close was where the two lavatories were located to serve the whole stair (the "R" was taken out of many a romance with nature's call), and of course the close was the entrance to the high-density tenements.

His gas at a peep

As a result of all this practice with my pal's brothers, both of us were quite accomplished dancers by the time we were fifteen years of age (we could even birl, which was considered a bit gallus). We were now equipped to enter the glittering world of ballroom dancing.

We soon discovered, however, that all was not well. Having paid our sixpences to get in, we girls had to stand like performing seals at one side of the hall, while the fellas stood on the opposite side eyeing us up and down, even condescending to "lift" us. The result was, if one was not in the dancing fraternity (or sorority) and not a proven rerr dancer, one could be standing there all evening without getting on the dance floor. What a terrible injustice! But wait a minute; there was a loophole.

The practice was that the band would strike up a dance, usually a foxtrot, tango or waltz; the fellas would then dive across the hall, grab their partners, and take the floor. There were two breaks during the dance when the band stopped. After the first break, one was allowed to split. This meant that either male or female could tap a couple on the shoulder and they had to split, and the tapper danced with one of them.

The snag was that one had to have a brass neck to pluck up the courage to do this. Since I worked in a printing factory, earning twelve shillings a week, the thought of some three hours hard work to earn my sixpenny admission fee for my evening's dancing quickly gave me a neck like a rhinoceros and all the courage in the world. Having got that length I wasn't slow at splitting. Not only that, I stood back and assessed all the male dancers and split the best dancer in the hall. Using this method I finally succeeded and was accepted into the dancing fraternity.

Other ploys were adopted, such as standing away out front to make it easier for the fellas to rush you on to the floor. However, it was a blue doo if they rushed right past and left you standing away out front like a real doo-lander. Another ploy was to rough up new shoes a wee bit to give the impression that old Twinkletoes had danced in every dance hall. The dance shoes which we used then, for some odd reason, were called Sahara Sandals. I have no idea why, since they had two-inch heels which would not be much good in the desert.

In those days the Glasgow dance halls were quite famous for running dance competitions. The next logical step, therefore, was to get right in there. My opportunity came one night in the Gordon Ballroom at Paisley Road West when I was invited by one of the lads to enter a tango contest (tango, no less!). And we got

. . . like a melody . . .

the length of the finals. My partner was a very nice lad and being a wee bit hen-toed he danced a good tango. However, he was unemployed (as were two million others) and didn't have a jacket and trousers to match, and we had an awful job borrowing a tie for him for the occasion. At least I was working. All the girls wore ankle-length dresses with big flowing skirts, usually made of voile or tulle, with sequins sewn all round the edges. My mother, who was a widow and cleaned offices and big hooses to earn a living, spent hours sewing the sequins round the yards of material.

That was life in Glasgow in the Thirties. Working people found relaxation and escape in the Glasgow dance halls. The result was that Glasgow was famous for its dancers. Then came the war, and a new era.

With the war, most young men went into the armed forces and most young women either went to the forces or munition factories. I started work in Rolls Royce and trained to make engines. Since the men of our age-group were now away and the Yanks and big bands became the social scene, the character of our dance halls changed, so also did our dancing. We all became jivers, and knocked our pans out jitterbugging all over the place (I got a guinea for demonstrating on one occasion) while working twelve-hour shifts day and night, six days a week. (*Heid doon, erse up!*)

But that is another story.

NO SEX PLEASE

THE QUHILK DAY the Magistrates and Towne Council, upon a supplication given in re John Smith, Dancing Master, allow and permit the said John to teach dancing within the burgh, with and under the provisions and conditions under written, viz.:—That he shall behave himself soberly, teach at seasonable hours, keep no balls, and that he shall so order his teaching that there shall be noe *promiscuous dancing of young men and young women together*; but that each sex shall be taught by themselves, and that one sex shall be dismissed and be out of his house before the other enters therein.

From a minute of the Corporation, 11 November 1699

CONCERNING GLASGOW MEN AND WOMEN

D. Macleod Malloch

ANCESTOR-WORSHIP is not much in vogue in Glasgow. In fact, ancestors are a little scarce; and a pedigree extending to three generations is considered highly respectable in commercial circles. Of course, it is not to be expected that the old landed aristocracy of Scotland would consider this kind of genealogy satisfactory; but money talks—in Glasgow as in America.

In consequence, those sons and daughters of commerce who are liberally endowed need not despair of marrying into aristocratic circles. As a matter of fact, some of them do so marry; and in doing so scale such giddy social heights that the event is not spoken of as a mere marriage. No. A breathlessly expectant world is informed that an alliance is about to be contracted between His Grace the Marquis of Owealot and Miss Janet Bigge-Pile, only daughter of John Bigge-Pile, Esq., JP, of Goosedubs Hall, and another address in Candleriggs which is carefully suppressed.

Upon such an announcement the great heart of the people is deeply stirred. Kelvinside trembles with suppressed excitement. Pollokshields gasps in envy. Bellahouston is openly jealous. In full knowledge of this blissful state of matters, John Bigge-Pile, Esq., JP, feels that he has not laboured in vain.

The brevity of the average Glasgow pedigree is hit off in the following story:—An old Scottish landed proprietor, or Laird, who piqued himself much upon his pedigree, and had a sovereign contempt for men who had come to fortune through successful industry, was one night in a company where a young lady from Glasgow happened to descant upon what her father, her grandfathers, and her great-grandfathers had done as civil rulers in the City.

After enduring this for a little, the Laird at last tapped the fair speaker gently on the shoulder, and said to her in an emphatic but good-humoured tone— "Wheesht, my woman; nae Glasgow folk ever had grandfathers."

The Book of Glasgow Anecdote

. . . and that laugh that wrinkles your nose . . .

THE CLYDE'S RED LEADERS

Jimmy Reid

UNTIL FAIRLY recently, a red-coloured lead preservative was widely used in the shipbuilding industry. On Clydeside, those who applied this somewhat noxious substance were known as—"Rid leedurs" or "Red Leaders" in the English, as it is spoke, in some places.

In the 1950s a Red Leader from Glasgow was refused a visa for the United States because his profession, as so brazenly admitted on the application form, was alien to the American way of life. The visaless red leader was a bit miffed. Steeped in the mystiques of craft trade unionism he was fair affronted at the very thought of red leaders being treated like pariahs while welders, platers and even plater's helpers were made welcome.

A workmate suggested that the Yanks might have thought he was a "Red Leader" as in a Red Revolution. This was pooh-poohed by the man deemed to be a dangerous subversive and serious threat to Wall Street, Blueberry pie, *Playboy* magazine, the Dow Jones Index and all the other venerable institutions in the good Ol' US of A. "Everyone knows they're aw deid," was his retort. He believed, as do many others, that once upon a time Clydeside was hoaching, not to say teeming, with Red Leaders who had failed, but gloriously so, to lead a successful revolution. Nearly all of them are dead, a necessary precondition for the deification of revolutionaries. So now we have academics, intellectuals, those in the media who are very partial to dead militants and that motley shower of verbal gunslingers who frequent the literary salons of Edinburgh, taking up, as their latest fad the "Red Clydesiders".

But was Clydeside as red as it's been painted?

One thing is certain. No "revolutionary situation," as defined by Lenin, Trotsky or anyone else, existed in the West of Scotland, during or after the first World War. Clydeside, a massive concentration of heavy industry, was overwhelmingly working-class in character. This generated a highly developed sense of class consciousness. It was therefore, not surprisingly, an area of industrial militancy. Such militancy, by its very nature, is concerned with defending or improving conditions within the existing social framework. It is reformist rather than revolutionary. All the mass struggles associated with John Maclean, Willie Gallagher, Davie Kirkwood and the rest, fall into this category.

Yet the Red Clydesiders were revolutionary in outlook. They did exist and I knew most of them in their later years. They were militants who also preached the gospel of socialism. The workers revered the former while not quite accepting the latter. They were marvellous characters. On the platform they would argue a philisophical case for socialism. Off the platform poor people sought them out and asked for help and advice on almost every aspect of life. At one moment they would be explaining Hegel's dialectics and the next, how some tenants could get their landlord to unchoke the backcourt drains.

Every locality had its own homespun Red Clydesider. They were the products not just of an industrial but of a specific social environment. During my childhood, Sunday night open-air meetings were part of the Glasgow scene. There were "stances" all over the City, where people could get up and speak and argue the toss. There was no television and the pubs and the cinemas didn't open on the Sabbath. Some speakers could regularly attract many hundreds.

For example in my home patch, Govan Cross was the stomping ground of Peter Colin Blair McIntyre. He was an anarcho/communist which was no mean feat for the anarchists and the communists hated each other with an intensity which far exceeded their mutual dislike of capitalism. Peter was a one-man band. A rampant individualist who proclaimed the virtues of collectivism. Like all the other "Reds" of that time he was interested in everything—philosophy, religion and science were all grist to his mill and emerged from his treatment as self-raising arguments for Peter's highly individualistic brand of stateless socialism. I can vividly remember the scene. In the semi-darkness, hundreds clustered around Peter on his soapbox as he answered questions on anything and everything. He was an entertainer. Outrageously irreverent and despite all attempts to conceal it, very much in love with the human race. At the time he was also a non-drinker. Years later his wife died and Peter simply went to pieces, started drinking and became an alcoholic and killed himself with booze.

George McLeod also spoke at Govan Cross. He was a Presbyterian minister and a Christian socialist of encyclopaedic interests. McIntyre was scathing about religion and what he called "pie in the sky merchants". This was a bit unfair on the likes of McLeod whose Christianity was the very opposite of the "Holy Johnny" and "think not of the things of this world" approach we expected from clergymen. In the name of Christ he implored the poor to get together and help themselves to remove the causes of their poverty. He argued that the better off should help the poor in this mission.

In my youth most young left-wingers became vociferously anti-religious as a reaction to the political respectability of the Churches. They even had a song with the chorus—"Down with God the dirty old sod", which they sang to shock people. If he did nothing else McLeod made me immune from such infantile atheism. He told us that Christ was on our side which I considered good news as we needed all the help we could get.

George McLeod founded the Iona Community, became Moderator of the Church of Scotland, and has remained a lifelong pacifist and socialist. I consider him an adopted "Red Clydesider", and was very pleased to succeed him as the Lord Rector of Glasgow University.

Willie Gallagher was another truly formidable character. He was a Calvinist-Bolshevik which is not as incongruous as it might at first seem. The theology of predestination and the theory of economic determinism have much in common, particularly the certitude that their cause must ultimately prevail. Willie hated "demon drink" as did many of the old "Clydesiders". Chairing a meeting for

Solidarity lives at home

Gallagher was something devoutly to be missed. In my teens I once did so. It was murder. He was fidgety and impatient to get on his feet and speak. Then he was in his element. He would overrun his time not by a few minutes but by half an hour and more and throw the whole agenda into a mess. Mind you, the audience loved it, for he was a superb agitator and the chairman got the blame for not sticking to the timetable. I vowed never again. Time, however, is a great healer and a few years later I agreed to chair/compere a bi-centenary celebration of the birth of Robert Burns organised by the Communist Party in the St Pancras Town Hall, London.

Willie was to give the Immortal Memory aided and abetted by another old Scot, the Marxist historian, Robin Page Arnot. On paper it looked a good idea. On the night it was a disaster. Neither Willie nor Robin made any linguistic concessions to an audience of cockneys, middle-class intellectuals from places like Hampstead and a wonderful contingent of Jews from London's East End. After a while they had a kind of glazed punch-drunk look. At the end they were muttering isolated words—"Muckle, ilka, snash". The Duo went on for nearly an hour longer than scheduled. The programme was constantly being revised. Certain acts were being dropped or cut back. The lamentations were loud. It was my first taste of the artistic temperament. At one stage I wanted to go on and stop the double act but was told you couldn't do this to Willie.

There is absolutely no doubt that on these occasions Gallagher abused his standing as the Grand Old Man of British Communism. Yet he redeemed himself with rare and exceptional qualities. Willie was a working-class intellectual as were all the Clydesiders. He had read and studied Marx, something some so-called Marxists of today have manifestly failed to do. Gallagher's interests were wider than politics and political textbooks. He could also make a political point by the devastating use of humour. On his best form he could have an audience convulsed with laughter. Above everything else he was courageous, with the natural bravery of the born fighter made immense by a philosophy which claimed that triumph was inevitable. Undoubted courage and unquestioning certitude breeds an awesome fearlessness. This was Gallagher.

John Ross Campbell was without doubt the best read man I've ever met. He was also, in many ways, the wisest. JR as he was known long before Larry Hagman was a gleam in Mary Martin's eye, let alone an entrepreneurial oilman from Dallas, was by far the most liberal of the Old Clydesiders. He was a Euro-Communist long before the term had been invented. He would have been a natural in the modern Italian Communist Party. A small man with large glasses behind which his eyes twinkled, he looked like an erudite and charismatic Arthur Askey. He was very witty with a sense of humour which at times could be almost surrealist.

I once had lunch with him and Gallagher in a Covent Garden Cafe. At the time I was reading a book of essays by Carlyle. So we discussed Carlyle or at least they did, and then Frederick the Great. Suddenly JR launched an argument which sought to show how such things as haemorrhoids could play a more significant part in historical developments than was recognised by Marxists. He claimed that Napoleon was plagued with the old Farmer Giles and was stricken right at the height of the Battle of Waterloo. According to JR his generalship suffered, so did his judgement, and he was also rendered incommunicado for a prolonged and crucial period. Willie, who was taking this most seriously, expressed grave doubts as to whether haemorrhoids and such like could be accommodated within the Marxist theory of Historical Materialism. JR leaned forward and said, "Willie, there are more things in heaven and earth than are dreamed of in our philosophy."

Campbell had a chequered history. A First World War hero, he had won the Military Cross and lost both his feet. In 1924 he was tried in the High Court for inciting the armed forces to mutiny. The crippled war hero defended himself and quoted the then Prime Minister, Ramsay MacDonald, in his defence. The case was dropped.

He was, among many other things, an economist. His office was piled high with all sorts of reports, documents, books and magazines. His large desk was so heaped with paper, he had to stand up to see over. JR's method of sorting out or cleaning up his files was to cut with scissors any corner edges protruding from the heap.

JR Campbell was also brave. He had the bravery to doubt. His mind was always open to the possibility of being wrong.

Fiery man of peace, Lord Macleod of Fuinary

Peter Kerrigan was younger than the others. A big, athletic, handsome man from Springburn. A good footballer in his younger days, Peter was offered terms to sign for Rangers but turned it down because it would interfere with his part-time job as secretary of the Glasgow Trades Council. Peter was an engineer to trade and worked with Davie Kirkwood and Willie Gallagher. When he was describing things to you he would search his mind so as to get it exactly right. There was no embellishment. When he was wrong he was genuinely wrong and never dishonestly so. In this respect he was the most trustworthy of men.

Kerrigan had the reputation of being a hard man, a Stalinist disciplinarian. One Fleet Street paper actually called him "Butcher Kerrigan". I first met him in my teens and got to know him, very well, in my twenties. He was, without any doubt, one of the warmest-hearted human beings it's been my good fortune to come across. He was actually a gentle man. Maybe he had mellowed. It's true he had once shared Gallagher's aversion to alcohol until converted to its blessings by Harry Pollitt. The story Harry told was this. He and Peter were at a reception in London and Harry kept giving the big fella Drambuie and told him it was a rather strong brand of ginger beer. Anyway, Peter never looked back and enjoyed a good dram to the end of his days.

When Kruschev exposed the horror and bestiality of Stalin's regime at the 20th Congress of the Soviet Communist Party it had a traumatic effect on big Peter.

You see, he had been the British representative to the Communist International in Moscow in the late thirties during the show trials. He had known the old Bolsheviks who had been involved in the revolution of 1917. Three out of four had been tried and convicted and executed as foreign agents and counter-revolutionaries. In retrospect it might seem incredible, but Peter accepted the explanations about confessions and treachery. But before we start condemning, just remember the period. Fascism was on the march and Stalin or what he was supposed to stand for seemed the only alternative to many good people. The overwhelming wish to believe is the great master of self-deception. Peter used to recall with deep emotion his Russian comrades from the Spanish Civil War who had all been slaughtered in the Stalin terror. Kerrigan's honesty would never permit him the luxury of equivocation. He was bitter about R. Palme Dutt, the arch-apologist for Stalinism in the British Communist Party after the 20th Congress. He described the murder of millions as "a spot on the sun". Kerrigan, Campbell, Gallagher and for that matter Pollitt loathed Dutt and for reasons which were honourable.

The last remaining Clydesider is a wonderful old man called Harry McShane. As I write, Harry is in hospital, alive and kicking albeit a little feebly. He was the closest to the legendary John Maclean. He also retained certain independence of judgement which made him a little different. Could I put it this way; if Harry had been a Russian he would have been executed in the thirties. He was bound to kick over the traces, for McShane is a constant rebel. A natural nonconformist. He was combating Stalinism before Khrushchev's exposé.

Harry was one of the outstanding leaders of the unemployed m 'vement of the thirties. He was more effective as a debater than an orator. Like all the others he was well read. An erudite man who realised that real knowledge is on the side of the oppressed and ignorance a weapon for the oppressor. That's why tyrants always want to burn or ban and censor books.

This, I think, is what all the Clydesiders I've known had in common. They believed in the exercise of human reason, in the liberating potential of knowlege. To them socialism was supposed to be the emancipation of minds as well as bodies. OK, so some of them picked the wrong, the terribly wrong model, but this doesn't invalidate the intention. I think we still have a lot to learn from the "Clydeside Reds", including their mistakes.

A TOUCH OF GREENERY

Owen O'Leary

FOR STARTERS, THE very name Scot came from Ireland, and I have never in my life worked out why some people in this Northern piece of sceptred isle real estate should be shirty about the Irish in Glasgow, when, for God's sake, we invented the place.

What I am talking about is the invasion many centuries ago by the tribe the Roman scholars called the Scoti, who sailed across the water in coracles or something of the kind, from the actual Emerald Isle, and displaced the Picts, whose only

A broth of a bhoy

contribution to civilisation was some kind of heavy duty tattooing. God knows where the Picts came from, God knows where they went to, but God has better things to think about.

There are plenty of theories about where the Scoti tribe came from before then. A schoolmaster once told me the word was a kind of modification of Scythia, and that's where our tribe was born. Another schoolmaster, and what a boring old poof that one was, said that the name was given us by a Pharaoh's daughter, Scota. If you believe any of that, you'll believe anything; but in the case of the Irish, anything you believe is probably God's own truth.

There'll always be an Ireland

Glaswegians, who think history started with the formation of John Brown's shipyard and the arrival of St Columba, have no long-distance sense of history. Columba assuredly came to Scotland to rescue the place from its innate barbarity, and that is Irish enough, since he was a well-known tearway in Ireland and got out a few hours ahead of the posse, and turned himself into a nice genteel Christian gentleman on the Larne-Stranraer ferry, and was very nice to himself at the confessional for the minor sins he had committed back home.

But a lot of the Irish, God's own people, were quite content to stay at home and ignore all that wild colonial boy nonsense, because Ireland was the lost continent, full of accordeon music and football and whisky priests, till the eighteen-forties, when the sodden English imperialists invented the potato famine—the very first Westminster try at curing the Irish Problem. In the name of Christ, *we* weren't overpopulating the planet. They could have done it in India and saved the world a great many pot-bellied doomed darkie kids with a year to live at most. But Ireland was handier, I suppose.

So a lot of those that were left, left. For Glasgow, although being thoroughly Irish, they imagined they had booked passage for New York, and when they were pitched out of the holds at the Broomielaw, they tried to talk Gaelic with a Yankee accent, so as not to be mistaken for Cherokee and shot on sight. My own forebears did just the same thing, they came up the Clyde on a potato boat, and a lot of them got free passage by posing as potatoes, not too complicated an imposture for the Murphys.

They sank without trace. But there was another wave of invaders coming, around the turn of the century, because the English government did something else clever and the blessed island was too hot to handle, and we came over in our thousands—a word we could never encompass too easily, having only the routine number of fingers on our hands. And at that time, there were Throubles in Ireland, again for God's sake. The bold Fenian bhoys were out to nibble away at the substructure of English imperialism, and there were people in Westminster who could hardly stay awake for worrying about them. So the innocent Glasgow natives, who had no idea they had all come from Ireland in the first place, thought every thick Irish immigrant was a Fenian, with bombs concealed in every human orifice, and I can tell you, that would make a man walk very funny. John Wayne had piles, but a Mills bomb is just ridiculous.

And I will not hesitate to admit, because I am an honest man when you catch me napping, that a lot of us, my sainted grandfather included, couldn't read or write. All we could do was build canals and railways if you threw us a potato scone and shouted Paddy and used the whip. Even when we started to learn the English language, we spoke it right. We never said stair, we said sterr. We never said there, we said therr.

Have yez, or have you, ever wondered why so many good Glasgow pubs have names like O'Donnell's, or McCafferty's, or McIntee's? The reason my friends is simple. If you're illiterate, the one way you can climb out of the Glasgow gutter is by selling poteen; or the bookie business. The booze and the betting are the great levellers, and the Glasgow Irish could start buying over Bearsden by the simple

method of exploiting the weaknesses of this puritanical, Presbyterian city where
ministers shout about the wrath of God and hunger for a furtive tipple or a three-
cross double to get them out, for God's sake, from the dreariness of Knox's misery.
We never got into the brothel business because we thought a brothel was a soup
kitchen and there was no profit in that. But we're capable of learning.

And don't mistake it, a lot of us have. The sons and the grandsons, and even the
granddaughters, because unlike the English we like the female sex, have got the
grammar and the physics and the physique, and the law, and the accountancy, and
on a dark night they can pass for white. But don't get me wrong. It isn't the worst
place in the world for the Irish. If we missed New York because of a swindle by
some English shipowner, and we never were able to invent Tammany Hall, we
made our own in this nice wee town. Holy Mary, we own the Town Council, or
whatever they call it these days. You find me a Prod in the City Labour Party and
I'll show you a minority ethnic group.

And the Celts will always be a better team than the Rangers, believe me,
because there are Prods that support Celtic, but never a Fenian that would stoop to
supporting Rangers. Ah, the Irish are not going to take over Glasgow, they've got
enough of it to be going on with. And never mind what the priests or the Vatican
tell you, we don't fancy families of twelve kids either. I have two and I fancy neither
of them.

Tell you what, though. Glasgow without the Micks would be a damned boring
place, and a damned boring place is exactly what it isn't.

We never close. Queen Street, latish

GLASGOW NO. 7

Stephen Mulrine

When we wur wee
it wis aw berr feet
an who likes candy
an nane o yir cheek
an see us a lenny
an dreepin aff dykes
an kick-the-can
an shots oan bikes
wis rerr
When we wur wee
it wis holes in yir sannies
an egg-in-a-cup
fur tea at yir grannies
an sauce oan a piece
pit that in yir belly

K D R F
an chickie-mellie
dje derr?
When we wur wee
it wis durty rotters
an melt ye wan
an tears an snotters
an doggin it
an dae whit yir tellt
an single woodbines
an six o the belt
no ferr
When we wur wee
it wis ghosts an docs
an kuller earwigs

an big black clocks
an Ally Park
an hame tae yir maw
an Teeny Leek
an Heid-the-baw
wis therr
When we wur wee
it wis gaun yirsel
an honey perrs
an taste the smell
jis bein therr
wis gey near hivven
bit wee an aw
wis Number Sivven
ur merr

Charing Cross mansions and muses

CRITICS

Stephen Mulrine

No news is good news

Ah like a gude buke
a buke's aw ye need
jis settle doon
hiv a right gude read

Ay, a gude buke's rerr
it makes ye think
nuthin tae beat it
bar a gude drink

Ah like a gude buke
it opens yir mine
a gude companion
tae pass the time

See me wi a buke, bit
in a bus ur a train?
canny whack it
wee wurld i yir ain

Ay, ah like a gude buke
canny deny it
dje know thon wan
noo—whit dje cry it . . .?

Awright, pal, skip it
awright, keep the heid
howm ah tae know
yir trying tae read?

*

Wulliam McWulliam eh
whit a name
shoulda been wrut
in the Hall a Fame

No surrender
give us more
give us the Sash
my father wore

He staggers oot
tae the Walk hauf deid
a gammy leg
an a hole in his heid

Wulliam McWulliam eh
whit a haunle
wisht we hud him
in the Ludge Cardonal

*

Nsee that conductor
him an his botten
hidny a clue
shirricked um rotten

wavin his wand
tellin ye sum ferry
brung us in late
in the mizzererry

THE AGE OF ENLIGHTENMENT

Cliff Hanley

THAT WAS THE period up to the Forties, of course. Accept that mass unemployment imposed a level of deprivation hard to imagine today, with the visible fringe horrors of tuberculosis and rickets, that some people fulminated against the workless for dissipating their dole money on such luxuries as a wireless set. It was the age when Glasgow knew everything, or was within sight of knowing everything. It was the age of blessed certainty, which is now possessed only by people at the outer edges of politics.

And what fun it was. There were disagreements among us radical intellectuals, since there can be no dialectic without thesis and antithesis, and I wish I knew what that meant now. It was dazzlingly clear at the time. But the disputes were of form rather than substance, of organisation rather than ideals.

They were fierce enough, of course, and all the more fun for that. The Independent Labour Party, which had the received Truth, dismissed the Labour Party as having within it the seeds of its own destruction, and I regret that I recall only a snatch of a parody on "Keep the Home Fires Burning" which ran, "Stick to Marx my hearty, damn the Labour Party". The Socialist Party of Great Britain was no more than a splinter group of misguided Trotskyists, and the Communist Party was totally untrustworthy, though in moments of tension we would sometimes chant "Red Front". The others in turn saw the ILP as an endless tea party of idealist misfits, and we took some pride in that too.

The certainty of enlightenment had a lot to do with the giants that strode the land in that golden age, in direct line of descent from the saints, who started with Keir Hardie, the man who had done a Jericho act by turning up to take his Commons seat wearing a cloth bunnet. The walls hadn't totally collapsed yet, but it was only a matter of time.

John Maclean had a safe seat among the Blessed, and even the faintest reservation about either seraph was unthinkable. The ranks of the fiends were headed, not by a Tory, but by Ramsay MacDonald, who if not a fully qualified Satan was certainly a Judas who had opposed the General Strike of 1926 and headed a coalition government, and even called upon the King in fancy clothes and a sword.

In the meantime Red Clydeside had titans like Jimmy Maxton, Campbell Stephen and John McGovern.

It was permissible for insiders to smile now and then at the antics of John, though not for enemies of the people. John, it was said, would break *in to* prison to get his name in the papers; and he got it in with marvellous frequency. He knew what made headlines, and his contributions to Parliamentary debates made them every time. He didn't hesitate to clash head-on with the Catholic Church, of which he was a member, and it did look as if he did this so that he could have an equally dramatic reconciliation. The term "Honest John" was only mildly ironic, though, and the rumour that he had shares in a contraceptives company was probably libellous.

Anyway, his oratorical style was a fine frenzy of rabble-rousing, and splendidly exciting when rousing was exactly what we wanted. The red dawn suddenly seemed ready to burst in two days at most when he hit his stride, and he wouldn't have needed a microphone in Hampden Park, never mind Cranston's cinema. The fact that he went a bit funny later on and joined Moral Rearmament is not relevant here.

Campbell Stephen had been a Presbyterian minister, and doubtless the gentlest of shepherds. His hobby was taking more and more university degrees, which some of the comrades, especially those who read with their heads turning from side to side and their lips moving, felt might dilute his proletarian fervour, but as well as being rock-solid he was the most genial of mentors and an effective speaker in his own amiable style.

A then member of the SPGB (it does sound sinister, doesn't it?) called John Sinclair, who has since recanted, the rat, and now has long conversations with people like me and hardly ever mentions politics, considers that McGovern was the outstanding speaker of the trio, and doesn't remember being much moved by Maxton. It is, however, a scientific fact (and all our facts were scientific, society was a laboratory and we had the bunsen burners and the spectroscopes and everything all off pat) that Maxton had the authentic magic of oratory, from the stentorian barricades rallying call to a murmur that was never inaudible, because when Jimmy oped his lips, no dog barked. And he was funny. It is hard to explain this now, because if anybody else repeated his laugh-lines they didn't raise a smile. It ain't what you do, it's the way that you do it. The secret was personal magnetism, and few men in my experience have had more. To the faithful, Maxton had a Christ-like quality, and it becomes easy to understand the self-sacrificing fervour of the Apostles.

One could grudgingly admit that some people beyond the Pale of the ILP had a certain meretricious talent, even if they didn't have the received authority from the tablets of stone. Guy Aldred was an eccentrically glittering ornament of the Glasgow political scene; a one-man political party, or perhaps a one-man-and-a-boy party, because he was accompanied everywhere by a pale red-haired youth. He published a weekly called *The Word*, and that is about as definitive as you can get. It was put out by the Strickland Press, because, according to my information at the time, his lonely crusade for the ideal society was subsidised by the equally eccentric Lord Strickland (who later shot himself, but not necessarily for any reason connected with Guy) on condition that the paper should carry in each issue a plug for the noble lord's own particular crusade, which may well have been Flat Earth; and it did put in four or five lines reporting that Lord Strickland believed in whatever it was.

Guy was value for money, and nobody could be angry with him. He was burly and hook-nosed and never wore anything but a brown dog-tooth check knicker-bocker suit, maybe with the idea of wedding the past to the glorious future, or maybe because it was the only suit he owned. He was not given to frivolities of

A vanished Arcadia

fashion. He had a strong Cockney accent and a totally integrated belief in himself. He was afraid of no man or thing. During the war I attended a meeting in Coatbridge where he was the invited speaker and he delivered the undiluted Socialist message, including the certainty that the war itself was the inevitable outcome of the inevitable Capitalist crisis, which can be solved only by a war to mop up the over-production of the system. To any tentative protests about the evil of Nazism, he trampled through the questioner. He was great, and he was absolutely certain. He was also a touch of colour in a pretty drab wartime Glasgow.

So was Oliver Brown, whom I then knew only from a distance as a poly-chromatic figure in Queen's Park on May Day. Oliver wore the kilt and rode a bike to his job as a schoolteacher, come hail, rain or earthquake, and I think he left the Scottish National Party because there were too many people in it. He founded the Scottish Socialist Party, which appeared to comprise seven or eight young acolytes standing round his soapbox, and the strong inference was that if their number swelled to ten, he would chuck it and form another party in case his individualism was eroded. This should not be taken as derogation of a delightful man of gentle manners and enormous erudition, an incurable scholar who revealed to me for the first time that the Stuart dynasty was descended from pig-herds, the name being a modification of sty-ward. It is possible that the word was stig-ward, keeper of the hall, but sty-ward is much more appealing.

It is a matter of deep regret that I never heard Harry Pollitt, also classed by contemporaries as one of the great speakers of that golden age, Communist or no. (I believe Lenin was a lousy speaker. He must have had other talents.) I did avoid Harry McShane—oh boy, I'm telling you, ILPers were worried about Reds under the bed, just as the Communists fretted about ILPers under theirs. Harry is, of course, whatever his Communist experience, a small "L" liberal who believes in the unquenchable human spirit, and has one, thank God, or thank Marx, or whomever.

The Anarchist Federation was naturally a joke. Marxist theology has it that Socialism will graduate to Communism, which will graduate to anarchy, where laws are no longer necessary because man has achieved his full stature and dispensed with the authority of the withered-away state. Nevertheless, we laughed at the anarchists; because, possibly, they were trying to leapfrog the process; maybe just because they weren't in the ILP where we had got the whole thing dead right. The story was that when the anarchists got a band together to lead them on the May Day march, everybody played a different tune.

My only contact with this intriguing mob was during the Second World War, when the patriotic police were taking a sudden interest in Eddie Shaw, the anarchist leader—no, no, no, they didn't have leaders; the anarchist spokesman, maybe. I was a young reporter assigned to track down and interview this monster, who was believed to have lodgings in Queen's Drive. It turned out to be one of those experiences that make you wonder about coincidence and divine inter-vention and other matters which have no place in Socialist philosophy.

I took the tram to the foot of Victoria Road, looked at the massive tenement to the right, and set out to knock on every door to ask if anybody had heard of this dangerous subversive. At the first close, I decided to start on the top landing and work down. I knocked the door on the left and asked the man who answered if he knew the whereabouts of Eddie Shaw.

"I'm Eddie Shaw."

I forget what we talked about, but I do remember one of the nicest men I had met; and my boss had been right to assign a conscientious objector to the job. Eddie

Gone, all gone

and I had no quarrel at all. It shook me slightly to discover that members of other left-wing mobs were actually comprehensible human beings; because what I realise now is that out there on the left-wing we were all living in closed societies, nearly like monastic orders.

With mentors like Maxton and Stephen and McGovern, of course, it was hardly necessary for the comrades to think at all, never mind argue. And we hardly ever questioned the rectitude of the established church to which we belonged. But it was Glasgow, for heaven's sake. Argument was the staple industry.

We never noticed the dinginess of the wee ILP halls, in places like Shettleston and Tollcross and Bridgeton. They glowed with revelation; and they flowed with tea, of course. The Revolution would come on the crest of a tidal wave of tea. The tolerant comrades were a bit miffy about backsliders who indulged in a dram, and at one Burns Supper in Shettleston, the Immortal Memory was toasted in Iron Brew, a thing of which the Bard would hardly have approved.

But attending branch meetings was never a chore, it was an intellectual orgy. We endlessly and joyfully explored the mechanics of the revolution to come, and the glittering nuts and bolts of the ideal society it would engender.

Some things were too clear to need discussion or exegesis. The Theory of Surplus Value is unanswerable, for a start. In simplified form for slow readers, it goes like this: we have Capital on one side and Labour on the other. Labour is employed by Capital and produces goods worth £100 (Labour being the only true wealth). Capital, however, abstracts £30, leaving Labour deprived of its full reward, and overlooking the fact that Labour is also the consuming public. Labour now can't afford to buy all the goods it has produced, the classic Capitalist crisis of over-production has come, and the system collapses next Tuesday in a wanny.

The logic is so absolute that no time was wasted on discussing it. We picked nits over minor details. Talking is what we did. After a branch meeting, or a dance, or a night at the pictures, two or three kindred spirits would walk out, and two would walk the third all the way home, because there was something to be argued. Once outside his home, the talk was nowhere near finished, so two would walk the second home. If he lived five miles away, fine. The voices were lowered by this time, because it was well after midnight. If there were fine points still to be examined, two would walk the first home . . . and even repeat the circuit. We didn't sleep a lot. We talked.

On the question of how artists would fit into the brave new world, I had the obvious answer that although they weren't real producers of wealth in the basic sense, not genuine members of the proletariat, art was quite nice, and apart from people doing it as a hobby, talented limners would be selected by a government committee and allowed to do it full time. I was brilliant, I tell you. One of the other comrades, a real fink, argued that the artist would not be cribbed or confined by government committees, and if that was my attitude he was taking his ball home and the game was a bogie.

We got the place of sex in society sorted out too, more or less. Being hot-blooded teenagers and desperately frustrated, and having read Bertrand Russell on Sex and Society, we framed a law making the whole thing free for all. We didn't actually consult any female Socialists to find if they fancied giving it to anybody who asked. In an ideal society they would enjoy it just as much as we hoped to.

Anyway, in that ideal society, everybody would be pretty nice, and probably tall and handsome or petite and cuddly as well, not to mention being able to speak fluent French and sharp at maths and chemistry, and Esperanto, whatever that was. There was never any problem about matching this to the people we actually knew. One of the ILP branch secretaries had been discovered dipping into the till, and a left-wing councillor or two were doing time; there were some members who, it was generally agreed, were thoroughgoing poultices. But when Socialism came, they would be transfigured. And there would certainly be a lot of sex.

Russia was already the ideal society back in the Thirties, even for non-Communist left-wingers. The treason trials over there were simply Capitalist propaganda. The Five Year Plans were masterstrokes, and it was significant that of all three European dictators . . . sorry, leaders . . . Stalin was the one who smiled and was therefore a nice man.

We even toyed with the idea of Glasgow declaring UDI and becoming an independent soviet republic, with free transport, food, swimming baths, rent, and certainly sex.

Don't knock it, because I am not knocking it. It genuinely was the age of enlightenment, it was the age of certainty. It was the age of Glasgow's dream, and the dream was stronger in Glasgow than anywhere else.

And that is truly the golden age. The golden age is not when everything is perfect. It is the age when we believe everything can be perfect. My generation has lived through the golden age, and I am glad of it.

Where was Harland and Wolff, again?

TOM JONES IN GLASGOW

Billy Sloan

IN 1983, WELSH superstar Tom Jones embarked on his first British concert tour in over ten years. I caught his show at Glasgow Apollo, and was impressed by his still powerful tonsils and explosive, sex-charged stage show.

Most of the audience were tipsy women—quarter bottles neatly concealed in handbags—who were determined to have a rerr terr and a good ogle. As Jones whipped off his jacket, exposing his he-man hairy chest and thrust his hips provocatively towards them, the excitement level reached fever pitch. His tight clothes left nothing to their imaginations. Then with 3,000 females simultaneously bursting a blood vessel, one of them rushed up to me and, in a mixture of ecstasy and obvious distress, screamed into my ear.

"Wid ye just look at that boady. He's the only singer in the wurld I'd haud in a pee fur . . ."

Only in this fair city could twenty years of gold discs, Las Vegas sell-outs, phenomenal riches and international acclaim be summed up by the self-discipline of a wee Glesga wummin's bladder movements.

John Knox does not budge an inch

IT'S A GAELIC GLASGOW

Donald McDonald

> *When I came to Glasgow first*
> *A mach gu tir nan Gall,*
> *I was like a man adrift*
> *Air iomrall dol air chall.*
> *Am fuaim a bh'aig an tramway car*
> *Was rumbling in my ears*
> *Is nuair chaidh mi sios am Broomielaw*
> *My eyes were full of tears.*

IT WAS A clever Lowland fellow who told me that this verse was "a superb macaronic derivative". I sagely agreed with him and offered to buy the next round. As he was a lecturer in social sciences he ordered an obscure whisky that no self-respecting Gael would contemplate as drinkable. I bought it for him anyway. Why let him into the secret that the Gaels know more about Glasgow . . . and whisky . . . than they would wish to let on to anyone?

The Gaels must have a strong claim on Glasgow because they named it. Angus Matheson, the first occupant of the Chair of Celtic Studies at Glasgow University, proved fairly conclusively that the city's name came from the Celtic words for

The world's greatest trading nation

"grey river" and that seems to me more convincing than any case for a dear green place, however many literary awards the latter can gather. After all, didn't Angus have a prodigal brother who become Professor of Celtic at Edinburgh University?

The Gaels have probably been coming to Glasgow since they named it. One of the many historical myths about the city is that we did not come here until after Charlie's year or the first potato famine. It is a myth easily laid to rest. St Columba Church in St Vincent Street has had the good sense not to consign its records to fashionable archives in Edinburgh and consequently documents are still available for those who wish to read, touch and feel history. St Columba may now be Scotland's Gaelic Cathedral but in 1769 it was established as the Gaelic Chapel in Back Cow Lane.

Even the address was significant . . . the terminus of a long drove road from the north. More significant, perhaps, is the list of those who petitioned the Council and the Bailies to set up the congregation. Over one hundred of them were already established businessmen in the city: innkeepers; ostlers; dry-bleachers; spirit merchants; drysalters; farriers. Obviously they had not got there overnight. Touchingly, there are some on that original list who described themselves as "refugee" or "fugitive". In the year that the Chapel was established there were 20,000 people in Glasgow who could speak only in Gaelic. Monoglots, my friend from the social sciences would have called them.

Perhaps we came early because this is a welcoming, mongrel place of a city. A sort of international lucky-bag. What kind of racial one-upmanship could you ever exert when a Lithuanian Jew meets a Skyeman in a shop run by a Kerryman in Argyle Street? Perhaps their accents made them realise they were all in this mess together. And it was a mess!

I only came to Glasgow in the twilight of its great days; the era when it was moving from being the second city to a place in the second division. Like the macaronic poet I was "like a man adrift". But when no danger threatens, what a pleasurable thing it is to be adrift! In my anecdotage I still remember the erratic neon signs, the defaced war victims (where did *they* all go?), the pavement artists on Jamaica Street, the houses that were ticketed to declare that only two and a half people could live there; the new experience of Orange bands and Walks that needed an explanation and with always someone there to provide it, the ferries across the river where your accent could pay your fare, the late-night coffee stalls in dim, exciting streets that I have never been afraid to walk.

Perhaps most important of all was that you were given a welcoming, universal name. As some forgotten poet put it:

> *I'm Jimmy the punter from Partick,*
> *I've lived with this name all my life.*
> *And now all my weans are called Jimmy*
> *And Jimmy's the name of the wife.*

And when the eyes got misty for the Hebridean sunsets we would rather dream about than actually see, all we had to do was take a stroll beneath the Umbrella on a

Don't jump!

Saturday or a Sunday night. The queers and the ladies of the night occupied one pavement below the Central Bridge: the Gaels occupied the other. Who am I to say that the twain never met?

A city of blancoed tenement stairs; a city of shipyards that built men as well as ships; a city of back-courts where the Monday morning claim to a stretch of washing line was contested with the intensity of a Culloden field; a city where pubs could call themselves Dirty Dick and still get customers; a city where tramps on the benches at Anderston Cross could talk, with authority, about temperatures in the Yukon and the habits of sheep in Queensland. I'm glad I got here one step ahead of the bulldozers.

Like all the other Gaels I came to Glasgow for education and for work. Today I am a Glaswegian by choice. I've now been here most of my life. I intend to spend the rest of my life here. Although I am a parochial, insular man, I have lived for spells in other cities as diverse as Hamburg and Minneapolis. Home is still for me an isolated croft in a remote community of the Western Isles. Glasgow is the place where I *choose* to stay.

It has been my university. It bred in me anger about injustice and inequality; it gave me my politics from the eccentric soapboxes of Guy Aldred and Harry McShane; it taught me a sense of community living from the sometimes claustrophobic realities of tenement existence; it acquainted me with violence through the gangs of Partick and Maryhill and that only because I was too young to know Billy Williamson and the Cumbie; it gave me a folk-identity with the gallant losers like

This stuff grows on you in this town!

Benny Lynch, Jackie Paterson, Matt McGinn and a thousand others who in beating the system were destroyed by it; it germinated the awareness that places like Bearsden and Giffnock are as much ghettoes as the Calton and the Gorbals were, but that the latter had possibility on their side and the former were damned by their own complacency; and, without the benefit of a Greenwich Village or a Left Bank, it introduced me to writers, poets, artists, comedians and actors . . . there were a dozen of them in every street I lived in! Glasgow for me is a city that never was mean.

Yet the Calvinist in me comes out. It's probably a male-menopausal thing but I now think of Glasgow as a city with a wonderful future behind it. The bulldozers, and their allies, the planners, have destroyed something of the excitement and the freedom that was Glasgow. The developers are throwing up ticky-tacky houses designed to make people keep themselves to themselves. Anderston Cross and Gorbals Cross are gone. Partick Cross is a castrated, affordable compromise. The Saracen Head is a tourist attraction.

When I recently mentioned Queen's Cross to my son, who lives in Possil, he looked blank and then accused me of always talking about crosses we have to bear. In that lies the ultimate irony about Glasgow. St Michael-suited planners who live in Houston and Mugdockbank have got rid of our crosses . . . the place where the vertical and the horizontal meet . . . and given us dampness and condensation instead.

The real joke is that they think they've got away with it. Just let them wait! The revolution is coming tomorrow . . . isn't it? And sure Glasgow is still the greatest, friendliest city in the world . . . isn't it? You'd better say yes or I'll kick your teeth down your back throat. It's my type of town.

> *"Tha iomadh bliadhn bho'n latha sin*
> *I'm in Glasgow till this day,*
> *'S an coibhneas mor ri'm choimhearsnaich*
> *I ever more will stay."*

I'll say amen to that.

THE DISCOUNT HOLIDAY

A New Play by Michael Kelly

The curtain rises on the departure lounge of Alicante Airport. It is the early hours of the morning and the airport is deserted apart from 112 Glaswegians waiting for their flight home after two weeks in the Rio Park Hotel, Benidorm.
*   Two of the returning holidaymakers,* JESSIE *and* SADIE, *are walking slowly*

A Provost and his peer, Kelly and Mack

Twenty-six miles? A cakewalk

from the duty free shop, each with a plastic bag in her right hand. JESSIE *is also carrying a large stuffed green donkey and* SADIE *is wearing a straw sombrero. They wear cotton print dresses and white cardigans. They are followed by a young, handsome, sunburnt, well-dressed, red-bearded man of whom they are unconscious.*

Above the strains of "E Viva Espana" sung by the younger members of the group the women converse.

Jessie: Haw Sadie, there's thone photos they took when we got off the plane.

Sadie: Aye but our's is no there. They've missed us.

Jessie: That's typical. They're supposed to take everybody so they can have a souvenir. I'll bet a' they Germans got one.

Sadie: Aye. Were you going to buy one, Jessie?

Jessie: Buy one? I wouldnae give them the money. But they should be there. They cannae dae anythin' right.

Sadie: Still it was a rerr holiday. What a great hotel!

Jessie: Aye, but 'am no takin that room again. It was above the deep-freeze.

Sadie: Aw, wis it cold?

Jessie: Naw it wisnae cold but it kept shakin'. Still it wisnae as bad as Sammy's. He was above the kitchen. Couldnae sleep for the heat.

Sadie: Aye, but yous'll get money back from the travel agents for that and you can go away for the September weekend.

SADIE *turns and notices that the man following them and who has been listening intently is* MICHAEL KELLY *the youngest Lord Provost Glasgow is likely to have.*

Sadie: Hey, it's Kelly. Sure it's Kelly. Are you Kelly?
Kelly: Well . . .
Jessie: Naw, it's no Kelly. Kelly's got black hair. You're no Kelly.
Kelly: Well, I am. And my hair's red.
Jessie: Naw it's no. I've seen you on the telly and your hair's black.
Kelly: But you've got a black and white telly.
Jessie [*suspiciously*]: How did yu know that? You're no Kelly.

The airport tannoy interrupts, announcing a four-hour delay in BX111A to Glasgow. SADIE *and* JESSIE *slump into a couch, grimly smug expressions on their faces, and begin to calculate the further rebate they intend to claim.* KELLY *stands deflated and lost.*

Curtain.

DEAD HONEST

D. Macleod Malloch

BROADLY SPEAKING, Glasgow has been fortunate in its civic rulers. The breath of scandal seldom has attached even to a Councillor—let alone a Lord Provost or a Bailie. The wholesale graft which is apparent in American Municipal Politics has no place in this happy city; or if it has a place it is an obscure one.

True, one has heard from time to time rumours of corruption upon the licensing bench, and stories have been circulated regarding the profits to be made even by a common Councillor. But these things have seldom, if ever, been authenticated. Even if they have been done in secret they have certainly not been proclaimed upon the housetops. Therefore the Glasgow citizen pays his rates with resignation, and comparative punctuality; satisfied that he is getting better value than is vouchsafed to ratepayers in less favoured communities.

He may begrudge the Edinburgh man his Princes Street, and the general beauty of his city. But a consideration of the Edinburgh tramway system speedily restores the Glasgow man's equanimity. Or having imbibed Talla water in Fair Edina, he can turn to "pure Loch Katrine", satisfied that he has also in this respect the better of his Eastern Brother. Indeed, generally speaking, Glasgow has been and is a well-governed city, and its list of Lord Provosts is a roll of which the city may justly be proud.

The Book of Glasgow Anecdote

Suddenly naked

AN ADOPTED BAIRN

Lavinia Derwent

I WAS BROUGHT up with Clydesiders but not in Glasgow. They had four legs and muckle long tails. Indeed, *muckle* was one of the first words I heard. "Ye canna ride on that muckle beast's back." "I can so!" It was a long way to fall down. Easier, I found, to plait their tails and tie them with red ribbon. "Daft lassie!"

So I felt akin to Glaswegians when I became one of St Mungo's adopted bairns, though I had as many falls off the shoogly trams when they whisked round corners as I had off the Clydesdales. The trouble was that I arrived in a fog and remained in one for many a long day. "Do I turn right or left?" I was always asking. "Depends where ye're gaun, lassie!" So I went straight on till I bumped into something.

Now, of course, Glasgow belongs to me, and I am constantly directing strangers to turn right, left or centre. But I was stumped the other day when a lorry-driver yelled at me, "Which way to the palace?" "What palace?" "Where the Queen bides. Where is't?" "D'you mean Holyrood?" "Ay, that'll be it." "Wrong town," I told him and directed him to Edinburgh. I hope the Queen had the kettle on when he arrived.

We all know how beautiful the environs of Glasgow are, but never on the day visitors come to admire Ben Lomond. "It was lovely and sunny yesterday," I protest, peering through the mist at the invisible Ben. But they go away with the firm conviction that it always rains in the West. Similarly, they are disappointed not to see razor-scars on my face. "I got away!" I tell them.

The truth is, it is no use having a one-night stand in Glasgow. One has to have more than bed-and-breakfast before savouring the special ingredients that make up the "Sauchiehall Stew".

I thought that a very strange name when I first heard it from the drawing-master at Jedburgh Grammar School. I hated the drawing-master. I couldn't draw for toffee, so Mr Thing made me into still life, and I had to sit on a stool in front of the class while they stuck out their tongues at me and drew dreadful pictures. Mr Thing was the first person I knew who came from Glasgow and was constantly talking of Sauchiehall Street as if it was heaven. "I'm going to hell," I comforted myself. Who wanted to meet a drawing-master in heaven?

But in the event I liked Sauchiehall Street when I learned to spell it, and loitered at every shop window. They were so different from the Jenny A' Things at home, with only a pair of stays, a packet of Abernethy biscuits and Bella's cat on display. What worried me were the street artists sitting on the pavements sketching Sunset in Rothesay Bay in coloured chalks, only to be washed away when

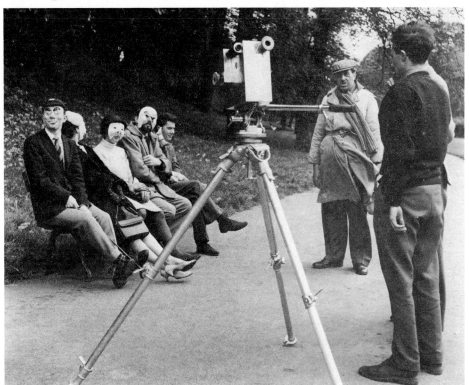

The Botanic's full of Faces (a film by Eddie McDonnell)

a shower of rain came on. I had a quick look to see if Mr Thing was one of them—
he wasn't—and was sorry I couldn't contribute to every hopeful hat waiting for
largesse. Many a time I had to take a devious route when my purse was toom.

My first lodging was a bed-sittingroom in Holland Street. It looked out on a
back green where I had non-stop "turns" from performers with bad colds who
coughed pathetically while catching coins wrapped in tishy-paper. There were
times when I had to harden my heart and draw the blind, else I would have been
forced to join them in their raucous rendering of "Annie Laurie".

One darned hing after another

The picture-houses intrigued me. At home we had only the silent pictures,
once in a blue moon; not so silent when the reel broke down and we gave the slow
handclap. "Why are we waiting?" Miss What's-It played hurry-up music on the
tinkly piano and we clapped faster to keep pace with her. But here the film stars
spoke and a gentleman in evening dress rose up from nowhere seated at the
mighty organ and played magic music without coughing or expecting tishy-paper
money. I went home, bemused, to my bed-sittingroom and thought I was fairly
seeing life.

Hearing it, too. After seeing no crowd bigger than a flock of sheep and hearing
no louder sound than the whaup's, the dirdum of the traffic and the jostling of
passers-by on the pavements left me fair bamboozled. I could have stood and gaped
at them for ages. But I had to explore my new surroundings. I was told that
Provand's Lordship, the oldest house in Glasgow, was well worth visiting. But
where was it? "In Toonheid," I was told. So I got on to a tram and asked for a ticket

On the outside looking in. Glasgow Green

to Toonheid. "Awa' hen! ye mean *Townhead*," reproved the conductress. But once there, nobody had heard of Provand's Lordship. "What is't ye're lookin' for, onywey?" a wifie asked me. "It's the oldest house in Glasgow," I told her. "Come on up oor close," said she, without batting an eye. "I'm livin' in it. Hasny had a lick o' paint for years."

This was my first introduction to Glasgow repartee, but not my last. On the top deck of a bus when I was flung on to the lap of a wee working man, he took one look at me and said, "Awa' hen! ye're no' ma type."

It was in Townhead, too, that I saw my first hinger-oot. She had it reduced to a fine art. Up with the window, out with the cushion, settle on the elbows, open the mouth. "Hi, Geordie, what's new?" She was a talking-picture in herself.

It was only when I came to West Nile Street that I felt a trifle homesick. I stood watching the poor plodding horses with sparks flying from their feet, sliding back on the slippery cobbles. I longed to run after them, plait their tails and set them free in the hayfield at home. But maybe they did not want to be transported to alien territory. After all, they were Clydesiders.

Me, too. I was no longer an adopted bairn. *Ich bin Glaswegian.*

JUSTICE

D. Macleod Malloch

A BOY WAS brought before a Glasgow magistrate charged with stealing a handkerchief from a gentleman's pocket. The indictment having been read, the Bailie, addressing the boy, said:—

"I hae nae doot ye did the deed, for I had a handkerchief ta'en out o' my ain pouch this very week; sae ye maun gang to the jail for sixty days."

The Assessor here interposed, stating that the case had not yet been proved against the boy.

"Oh, then, in that case," said the worthy Bailie, "I'll just gie ye thirty days."

But on being again informed that even this sentence was contrary to law, he finally disposed of the case by saying:—

"Weel, my lad, the evidence seems a wee bit jimp this time, so I'll let ye aff; but see and no' do it again."

The Book of Glasgow Anecdote

Landscape with figure

The monsters are coming

THE OTHER SECOND CITY

Craig Samet

A LITTLE OF my history first of all. I came to Scotland on the strength of a romantic interlude in New York. I knew a girl there, and I came to Scotland. It's complicated. I came here during the great postal strike, so I couldn't warn anybody in advance, and I had to take pot luck. Being too lazy to learn a language, but hoping to work on a newspaper, the only logical thing was to come to Britain. Yes, it was all complicated.

I landed in Edinburgh a week before the Edinburgh Festival, and stayed in the YMCA, where I had a window overlooking the Edinburgh office of the *Glasgow Herald*. It was like looking into the stage set for "Front Page". Newsroom, 1930s. I finally played hookey from the YMCA, because they locked up at ten o'clock, and went down there one night, and made friends with some of the guys. I talked my way into writing the Fringe reviews for the *Glasgow Herald*. Three weeks in the country and writing reviews for the *Glasgow Herald*!

After that I had a vacation while I wondered what to do, and Radio Clyde came on the air. I thought this was an opportunity not to be missed, because if I had been around fifty years before, when commercial radio started in America, that would have been my game. I was fifty years too young—though I grew up around it because my father was in advertising. So I applied. And 475 other folk applied as well, but I was the second newsman they hired. So I was working in Glasgow, but I still lived in Edinburgh.

This is when I realised things were different East and West. I had made an occasional visit to Glasgow, and young people I knew—college kids in Edinburgh, deadly serious, would warn me, "Be careful in Glasgow, you never know what you'll find", "tough town", you name it. But this never existed; the town was new, it was dynamic. When I started working for Radio Clyde and going back to Edinburgh at night, it was like going into the wrong end of a funnel. I really felt things getting darker and darker as I went East in the train.

And as I got out at Waverley—you know what it's like getting out at Queen Street, you're in George Square, it's life, it's something happening—it did really feel like a funnel. That's when I realised Glasgow was so like Chicago, where I came from. Since then I've realised there are so many historical connections between Chicago and Glasgow. Chicago has always been called the Second City, for instance. That seems to be lost in antiquity, but the reason, I'm pretty sure, dates from the time a man ran for mayor in Chicago to make Chicago the Glasgow of America. And he brought over the man who ran the Glasgow trams, which enabled the people here to become free. That's where the Second City came into it. People from Glasgow who go to Chicago feel at home, even though the American city architecture is so different. In the outskirts of downtown Chicago there are the older buildings that look like Glasgow buildings. And another thing the cities share—the reputation for violence—is a myth. Glasgow is a safer city than Edinburgh. I would rather be fighting a Glasgow gang than an Edinburgh gang, because Edinburgh gangs have no hope. Edinburgh isolates all the people like that away out in ghettoes, high-rises, while Glasgow is beginning now to bring life back into the city, the city centre is beginning to spread outwards, there's a sense of dynamism.

And Glasgow's always ahead in fashions. Like the blacks in Chicago—no matter what the problems, they always had the stylish, the outlandish clothes, they were the leaders. Here too. That's what attracted me. And because Chicago and Glasgow are so psychologically alike, I feel that place as a part of me. Crazy thing, I was supposed to be named after my great-grandfather, who was a Charles. My folks got as far as the "C" and ended up with Craig, which is a very Scottish name; and they still can't explain it. But there's some mystical connection between that and my being here. This is my home. When I go back to Chicago I'm a visitor, I don't feel at home till I come back here; much to the relief of my mother-in-law, because my wife is Scottish, and there's a certain fear that I'm going to steal her and transport her to America.

Glasgow people never look inward. They think about themselves, but their generosity always turns outward. Even my father, when he came here, and had to do the ritual tour in London, the Changing of the Guard and so on, found it a total disappointment. It was the first time he had been out of America, and he said he couldn't wait to get back to Glasgow. He had only known the place for two days.

I mentioned Radio Clyde, and the obvious thing about it was that it had an identity, because its audience had an identity. When Radio Forth started in Edinburgh it took two years to figure where it was going, and had to rejig everything, because nobody knew what the hell an Edinburgh person *was*. Glasgow people know what they are—even if you can't put it in words, it's there, like a continual song, like a Broadway musical going on all the time. Yes, that's it. Glasgow is music to my ears.

FEED THE HAND THAT BITES YOU

Clem Ashby

NATIONAL FERVOUR takes many forms. I admit I was born in London, so after more than thirty years I am still regarded as a foreigner; whereas if I had come from Saudi Arabia, the West Indies, Australia, Pakistan or China I would have been a welcome guest to my city.

However, although technically a Londoner, I promise that the blood in the veins of my mother and father was pure Scottish. So surely that must make me half-decent. Show business in Scotland has occupied more than half my life, and for me a very happy relationship it has been.

It started in 1946, when I was appearing in a production of *Macbeth* at the Playhouse, Oxford. An agent landed himself in my dressing-room after the show and asked me if I could interest myself in a visit to Glasgow, where a firm called Howard and Wyndham was anxious to engage a Shakespearean actor for a show called *Half Past Eight*. I think I could have been persuaded to say no thank you, but having just married a Scots girl who lived outside Glasgow, I decided a change of scenery could be a good thing for a month or two.

That decision changed my life, for I've been here ever since, apart from one or three brief sorties to the nether regions south of the Border. My initial function in *Half Past Eight* was to appear in historical sketches such as "Henry VIII", "Storming the Bastille", "Napoleon Crossing the Alps" and similar rubbish, which for some reason that eludes me even now, the producer thought provided entertainment.

Luckily, the comic in the show, Harry Gordon, took pity on me and started using me in comedy. The following year I was asked back, but before the season started I was again playing in a production of *Macbeth* —this time at the Aldwych Theatre in London; and during the last day of the run, I had a phone call from David Steuart, who with Marjorie Dence ran the Perth Repertory Theatre. He told me he had been in touch with an agent who had given him the name of four actors (mine among them), then, with typical Steuart charm said the three others were busy, so could I come up to Perth for three weeks.

I did, and stayed for nearly twelve years, alternating between *Half Past Eight* in the summer and Perth and straight plays during the winter—a continuity of employment which, to an actor, was untold luxury. And of course, it started the many happy years of working with comedians.

One of the oldest clichés in the theatre is, "Comedy is a very serious business". As with most clichés there is more than a grain of truth in it, because in the same way that a footballer is only as good as his last game, a comedian is only as good as his last joke.

Most comics are reasonably sane and serious offstage. Some are downright miseries. But luckily I have avoided that particular breed. I worked with Harry Gordon for ten years, with one season away with Dave Willis; surely one of the funniest men Scotland has produced, and also one of the most difficult, mainly because he never used or indeed possessed a script, and he was loth to rehearse. Whenever he was asked about this he had a stock reply: "Och, we'll jist run through it in the pub across the road."

Harry Gordon was the complete opposite, a script for everybody and disciplined rehearsals. He was the entire opposite to Dave in other ways as well. At the end of each season, members of the audience sent gifts, mainly to the star of the show, the comic. One year Harry was given about six cigarette lighters, and he asked various people if they wanted one. Dave was once given four fountain pens and he asked if anybody wanted to buy one.

At the end of my tenth year with Harry I signed a contract for the following

Get that bum out of here!

summer, but alas, Harry died before it arrived. Stewart Cruickshank, managing director of Howard and Wyndham, had to search for another comic. He settled for Rikki Fulton, whom he had seen in an Edinburgh Festival Fringe show, and Rikki told Cruikshank that he needed a male feed; to which Cruikshank replied, "You've got one, he's under contract."

So, as Rikki never stops reminding me, he didn't *choose* me, he inherited me, and was lumbered with me for seventeen years. But for me they were seventeen very happy years because Rikki is very easy to work with, and one of his great virtues is that, providing you stick to the main structure of a sketch, he doesn't mind other people getting a laugh. When Jack Milroy joined Rikki in *Five Past Eight* (as it had become known) his feed was Glen Michael, and Glen and I subsequently shared a dressing-room for nine years.

The first time Glen appeared in one of Rikki's sketches, he put in a bit of unrehearsed business which he thought might get a bit of a titter. It didn't. It got a full-blown belly-laugh; so much so that when Glen got back to the dressing-room he looked as if he had just been handed down the death sentence. "Oh hell," he moaned, "I never thought it would go that well. I'm going to get the time-honoured words, 'That was funny. You leave on Saturday'."

I tried to convince him that Rikki wasn't like that, but he wouldn't listen, until Rikki put his head round the door and said, "Glen, I didn't see what you did, but for God's sake keep it in."

At this time the show's producer was Michael Mills, now a TV director. He often press-ganged Glen and myself into the big production number, which we hated. For a start it meant rehearsing when we could have been playing golf, and it usually meant we had to sing and dance. Glen had a rough idea of these intricacies but to me, dancing is as foreign as the Russian language, and someone once suggested that there isn't a note on the piano that fits my voice.

So whenever Michael Mills was looking around to see who was available, Glen and I hot-footed it to the nearest pub until the casting was complete. But one morning as we stood at the bar, a hand was placed on our respective backsides and we were frogmarched out of the pub, through the stagedoor and on to the stage—not a word was uttered by Mills but we were never called Glen and Clem again. It was "those malingering bastards".

I have mentioned that Glen and I shared a dressing room. Neither of us was the tidiest of people in show business and at the end, or indeed at the beginning, of the evening (especially on Saturday when we had two shows) it was the routine pig-sty and we could never find anything. One night Glen had a quick change into the finale of the first half, which he opened with the company singing and dancing. I joined in later.

Glen couldn't find his shoes, so I said, "Here, take mine, I'll make do with yours". He did, but I had forgotten that I take size nine and he takes size six. After he'd gone I found his shoes and tried to put them on. My heels were sticking out at the back. I eventually hobbled on-stage, but I couldn't take an active part in the proceedings because of these bloody shoes. Glen was faring even worse in the execution of a high-class piece of footwork, because his left shoe flew right off and landed in the orchestra pit; at which point he threw in the towel, and came off-

A lost serenade

stage muttering something that sounded as though it might rhyme with bucket.

Jack Radcliffe was another comic who was easy to live with. He was a bit of a rogue, but very likeable, and he was friendly with just about every criminal in Glasgow. Given time, he could furnish you with almost anything you named. I was with Jack in a show which also included Jimmy Logan, and one night I was standing around the stage door getting a little air, when two gentlemen entered (CID, it transpired) and asked to see Jack. The stage doorkeeper departed, and returned to ask them if they would mind waiting for five minutes or so. Eventually Jack arrived and took them to his dressing room.

Jimmy Logan was on stage during these proceedings, and at the end of his act went back to his own dressing room. Having finished for the evening, except for the finale, he decided to take a shower. He pulled the curtain of the shower aside and discovered the entire area full of radios, TVs and assorted stereo equipment, placed there, of course, by JR for the duration of the visit by the CID.

To round off this brief and turgid extract from my theatrical years, I would like to thank all the artistes with whom I have worked and who have greatly enriched my life; also the public, to whom we owe our living. Thank you for many kindnesses, particularly during my years at STV as announcer and newsreader. The hundreds of letters from you all were marvellous to receive and are kept with great affection.

Finally, thank you for allowing this foreigner to live in this lovely country for so many years. I hope there will be many more yet to come.

(Oh, see showbiz? See wee catchings of the throat? But it's all for real.–Ed.)

PRE-PADDLER

Andrew McQueen

IT WAS LATE in the evening and quite dark, and the tide having reached full flood, the boat was ready to start from the Broomielaw. There was no wind, so the oars were resorted to, to assist the ebb tide in carrying her down. The river and harbour were not lighted in those days, and the skipper at the tiller peered earnestly into the darkness for some landmark that might indicate the vessel's position.

At length, as the first indications of dawn appeared, his eagle eye seemed to descry a familiar outline. "Noo, Tonal," he shouted, "shust give her some draws more; there's the Dumbarton Castle; she'll soon be at Greenock noo".

The increasing daylight soon showed that the skipper's eyes had deceived him, and that the vessel, strange to relate, was still at the Broomielaw. An investigation into the cause of this phenomenon disclosed that, as the skipper expressed it, "She had been rowin' a' nicht wi' thon boo'd airn thing in"—in other words, they had forgotten to raise the anchor before starting to row.

Echoes of Old Clyde Paddle-Wheels

POTTY TRAINING A LA CARTE

Raymond Gardner

I ONCE PENNED the thought that the worst thing that had ever happened to Scotland was the building of a bypass round Gretna Green, on the basis that if more folk had actually been forced to drive through the village fewer might continue northwards, thus leaving heather, heath, and hame to me and mine. After all, the great wilderness in Europe (*sic!*) can hardly be that if every other road is blocked by Wallace Arnold's merrie men, not to mention something not at all like a stagecoach, the roads in between being blocked by foreign-registered caravans.

Of course they didn't build a bypass round Glasgow, the good men and women of the Council, née Corporation, being of a somewhat Roman bent. This meant that the quickest way between two points was a straight line and thus the motorway ploughed straight through the city. The only problem was that the motorway had exits and from time to time, finding themselves in lavatorial need, total strangers were to be seen in our midst. Hey presto, Jimmy, we had an embryonic tourist industry.

Then along comes this chap called Kelly who lives in an area much bypassed by hawkers and circulars, not to mention the motorways, with the idea that it's high time we changed our image, and what better way could there be to do it than to turn Glasgow into a tourist city. Alas, but by the time he came up with his idea the gauleiters of George Square had knocked down all of Glasgow's most famous and best loved buildings—known to the rest of the world as the worst slums in Europe. Midnight mystery tours of the highways and byways of the Gorbals in Wallace Arnold's latest fleet of air-conditioned stereophonic Saracen cars were not to be.

Indeed there came amongst us men of the dark cloth and the large car, known to mere mortals as Public Relations and Advertising Executives. These were the men who had changed an entire culture from porridge to Readybrek overnight. These were the men who could take coals to Newcastle and even get folk to buy them. Verily verily I say unto ye that these were the sons of Saatchi and Saatchi, not to mention a Mr Struthers, and yea they could make the Clyde flow backwards and the Waverley sail upside down at the touch of a word processor or the tickle of a whisker.

An eye for the birds

And the words that they processed made the immortal refrain that "Glasgow's Miles Better". And the men of the dark cloth and the large car looked upon the multitude and the multitude smiled in gratitude. And they took their slogan to London and plastered it on the doors of taxi-cabs and half the population of the Embankment Gardens threw their cans of methylated spirits in the air and died of heart failure and the last words of the last man amongst them was, "This day they have taken our birthright from us, Jimmy."

Having nothing else left to sell, the men of the dark cloth and the large car began to market the Glaswegian. Glasgow, as we all know, is not a city of razor gangs, thugs, muggers and fog. It is a city of smiling friendly people—the fact that none of them can direct you for 500 yards through streets in their own patch matters not a whit—reformed razor gangs, discos and sunshine. Even the Houses of Parliament—sorry, City Chambers—positively gleam, though, in the manner of a Hollywood set, if you go round the corner it's a different story.

Having persuaded folk who should have known better that what we needed was tourists and their ilk the good man Kelly—who neither smokes nor drinks—remembered that Scotland's new, liberal, and highly civilised laws regarding the consumption of the demon drink put a positive kick in the Costa del Clydo. In fact there are so many extensions and extensions of extensions that some folk think that Glasgow is just one enormous hospitality tent with a few houses round the outside. These, by the way, are known as schemes.

Tourists like to drink. The result is that more often than not Sauchiehall Street of an evening resembles a horizontal Tower of Babel patrolled by multilingual Glasgow police persons, desperately trying to force a path through the blitzed foreigners so that Ma, Pa and the weans can catch the last bus to Castlemilk after a night out at the "pictures".

The other thing that tourists like is to spend money, so, fast on the heels of the men of the dark cloth and the large car came the men of the zoot suit and the small car with the big word "Turbo" emblazoned across its arse, sorry boot. These men are known to mortal folk as entrepreneurs and they began rebuilding the pubs and restaurants of Glasgow. This cost them a great deal of money. In fact it cost them so much that nobody but tourists and other entrepreneurs could afford to drink and eat in them.

In fact drinking in Glasgow's new style shops has become a little bit like the antique business in which dealers buy from dealers who buy from other dealers in such a way that the one cheque just travels round in a circle. Pub-wise, publicans buy from other publicans and so on until the cash goes the full circle and the chap who came in last goes bust.

Foodwise, we have the youngest chefs in the world and most of them seem to claim to have been trained at Gleneagles, the Savoy, the Dorchester or all three. Judging by the age of some of them, it must surely have been potty training. The food of course is *nouvelle*, though in this year of Our Lord it is more customary to describe the white plate containing the one white shrimp on a bed of one warm lettuce leaf as being of "nouvelle tendencies". Warm lettuce has indeed taken over from the honest mutton pie on the grounds of health and the grounds of profit, but mostly on the grounds of profit, since there is no limit to the potential cash yield of warm lettuce given the proper accompaniments of air conditioning, silver service and half naked waitresses with French accents who indeed did go to finishing school. That is to say, they finished school in Paisley.

There is only one problem. If we are what we eat, then Glasgow diners must suffer from gastronomic schizophrenia since the warm lettuce in the restaurant tends to get replaced back home by the hot pie. This is because Daddy gave Mummy a microwave just like the MacTavishes next door, and why cook when you can make waves wi' the MacTavishes, eh? It is also because Glasgow women do not eat out very often and have therefore not discovered the wonders of chilled soup, warm lettuce and half cooked canard. Or half cooked—sorry naked—waitresses, for that matter.

If you do not believe me then pop into any one of a dozen of Glasgow's latest eateries—I will not name them for fear of reprisals from teenybopper chefs and their ex-model (lodging house?) waitresses wielding cleavers—and count the sexes. In London no self-respecting businessman would be seen dead at a meal without a woman in tow.

Realising that Glasgow is a village, one enterprising entrepreneur opened the perfect restaurant where, he claimed, you could be sitting at one table with your friend whilst your wife was at another table with her friend and you would never see each other. He's wrong. There is one facility which we all must share, and I don't mean the cash point.

It might seem that there is no solution but to give the place over to tourists from Lancashire, Limerick and Los Angeles. One pal of mine, being both a businessman and an entrepreneur, has come up with the answer, the only problem being that you'd need to be both a businessman and an entrepreneur to do it. He travels abroad quite a bit and is a superb and intuitive cook. He actually dined in the Nova Park in Paris a while back and in this tabernacle of the warm lettuce actually asked if his children could have a plate of chips, by Jacques! They didn't throw him out, not least because he came from Glasgow. No, they just told him that they didn't have the *mise en place*.

By my sainted Larousse.

So he came back to Glasgow and bought himself a restaurant where you can have anything except warm lettuce. He even employed a French chef of more than forty summers who actually came from France not Bermondsey.

THE DUCK CLUB OF PARTICK—1810-30

John Strang

AMONG THE MANY rural villages which at one time surrounded Glasgow, perhaps none surpassed Partick in beauty and interest. Situated on the banks of a limpid and gurgling stream, which flowed through its centre; and beautified, as it was of yore, with many fine and umbrageous trees; and above all, ornamented with an old hoary castle, with whose history many true and many more fabulous tales were associated; and when to these were added its dozen or two comfortable and clean cottages, and its picturesquely planted mills, historically linked with the generous gift of the successful opponent of the lovely Mary at Langside,—all combined to render this locality one of the most favourite of suburban retreats.

It was, in fact, the resort of every citizen who enjoyed a lovely landscape, an antiquarian ramble, or a *mouthful* of fresh air—to which might be superadded, the certainty of getting a *mouthful* of something better, provided the visitor should have ever heard of the good things obtainable within the walls of its ancient "Bun-and-yill-house".

Such was Partick during the latter part of the last century, a period when there existed divers knots of individuals connected with Glasgow, who, inspired by the noble purpose of enjoying ducks and green peas in perfection, with cold punch in ditto, proceeded hebdomadally to indulge their gastronomic propensities at this picturesque village.

Among the many inducements which this locality offered to these united bands of kindred spirits were, the agreeable and health-inspiring distance of this

In carnival mood

common rendezvous from the smoky City—the picturesque appearance of the village itself—the refreshing flow of the limpid Kelvin, broken by successive cascades—the neat and comfortable character of the hostelry; and above all, the superior quality of ducks reared under all the known advantages that arise from the proximity which large grain-mills naturally afford for good feeding. To these inducements, too, was superadded the delicious manner in which the ducks were prepared for table, and which never failed to excite an appetite, which was only appeased after each guest had finished his bird!

Of these various groups of Glasgow gastronomes, there was one which, *par excellence*, was truly entitled to the appellation of the DUCK CLUB OF PARTICK, seeing that, during the whole season, when these luxuries were in perfection, and even after they became a little blasé, there seldom was a Saturday permitted to pass on which the several members of this social fraternity were not seen either wending their hungry way towards the well-known "Bun' house" of that village, between the hours of three and four o'clock, or returning therefrom "well refreshed" before "set of sun".

Since the departure of these worthies from the scene of their gourmandising glory, the "Bunhouse" of Partick has as much ceased to Glasgow gourmets to be the shrine of Apicius, as the Castle of Partick to be the haunt of the antiquarian limner.

Glasgow and its Clubs

The sweet and limpid Kelvin

RODDY

Eddie Boyd

THERE ARE certain events that, even in retrospect, appear so arbitrary and callous as to make one wonder how anyone with an IQ of more than twenty-five can possibly subscribe to the idea of a benign supreme being. This was one of them.

Certainly, the day had started promisingly. The dawn had had none of that queasiness that so often seems to be a kind of alibi for the hours that follow. It made its promise early and seemed disposed to keep it. By noon it had matured into a glorious day of high summer with just enough of a cool breeze to allow my Woolworth rambling roses to justify their description in the most languid way. We had gone into Dumfries early on, thus giving a body swerve to the mechanical juggernauts that trundle their lethal way along the A76, leaving anyone who survives thoroughly convinced that Small is Beautiful. Rising betimes had brought the expected bonuses of hassle-free parking and shops where there was room to move and where oxygen and good manners were not yet at a premium. When we returned to the cottage we were feeling pleased with ourselves if not actually smug. As we opened the door, the telephone began to ring.

Now, like many people of my age and background, I have a healthy abhorrence of the telephone. I hear nothing but the voice of sturdy common sense from those who declare that if God had wanted us to communicate with each other across vast distances, He (or She) would have created us with louder voices and stronger lungs or might even have experimented with telepathy. Good news will always improve with keeping, no news is good news and who needs bad news? Reluctantly, I picked up the receiver and identified myself. There was a moment of silence before a familiar voice replied, "This is Pharic".

He's crying, I told myself incredulously and the thought threw me. In my time I have reduced BBC producers to tears of sheer, homicidal rage but not one of them had actually *wept*.

"Roddy's dead," the voice said.

I hung up and I walked away, trying to distance myself from the telephone and the voice and the terrible news. My wife looked at me and her expression conveyed to me that she knew something appalling had happened.

"Roddy's dead," I told her and walked out of the cottage which had suddenly become claustrophobic. Outside, the sun was still beating down but it was only something burning pointlessly in space. There were swallows clinging to the telephone wire like little animated crotchets. Then I had the weirdest thought: if nightmares, why not daymares? So I went and called Pharic again, hoping that he would tell me that it was all a mistake, an unpardonable sick joke, a misunderstanding; but all he did was to confirm the bleak truth and we ended up talking about something else that was yet, essentially, the same thing.

"What about Pike?" he asked.

Pike was the main character in a series which I had written and which had been successful enough for the BBC to consider commissioning a second series. It was called *The View from Daniel Pike* and the eponymous hero had been played wonderfully by Roddy. Call me prejudiced, self-regarding, biassed or anything else in *Roget's Thesaurus*, I will still maintain that Roddy never did anything better than Daniel Pike, the street-wise private eye with his populist morality and his harsh, alluvial wit.

"We could get someone else," Pharic was saying. "Like who?" I asked. "We're agreed then," he said, surprisingly. "Pike is dead," I said and that was that.

The next day we set off back to Glasgow. On the road, just as you approach Balmaclellan, I had noticed, previously, a sign which was no more than a piece of wood nailed to a post and which indicated that the passer-by was in the vicinity of a place which I had thought for a long time only existed on a theatre programme. Robert McLellan, that most intransigently Scottish of Scottish playwrights, had written a play called *The Laird of Torwatletie* which had been put on by Unity Theatre and whose first performance, if memory serves me right, had been in Edinburgh on Hogmanay 1946. Now, on a piece of wood, shaped like a thick-

bodied arrow the word "Torwatletie" stood out, a reminder that the part of the
Laird had been played by Roddy McMillan. Now it had a kind of improvised
pathos like a sad cross on a battlefield.

It was raining in Glasgow, a small, grisly, nagging rain, lukewarm with
summer. We were living in St Vincent Crescent at that time, a long, lovely sickle
of buildings which had once, about a hundred and fifty years ago, been quite an
uppity place to live. Since then it had fallen on evil times, had been re-scheduled
for commercial development, then granted a reprieve and was on the way up
market once again.

You meet a nicer class of people at the Steamie

About ten minutes away from this born-again crescent, just off Argyle Street
is Dover Street where Roddy was born and brought up. In physical terms, the
distance is nothing, but psychologically and socially it is immense and must have
been even more so when he was a boy. Yet this distance was something that he
always refused to acknowledge and time and again I would see him driving round
the district, waving to some acquaintance of the old days, tooting the horn at some
ancient biddy who would screech a delighted welcome back at him.

This was not just the local-boy-made-good ensuring that everyone knew it
nor was it simply *nostalgie de la boue*. It was mutual recognition of integrity and
respect impossible to mistake or misunderstand. There was even something
euphemeristic in it, at least on Roddy's side. He was the giant Antaeus who was
invincible as long as he kept his feet on the ground.

I picked it this very morning

There were quite a few of these people at the memorial service which was held in Anderston Church. Someone more detached than I was capable of being would probably have found it a fascinating social mix. The famous rubbed shoulders with the forgotten, executives mingled with ex-Communists, people who travelled thousands of miles every year found themselves seated beside other people who, like the great philosopher, Emmanuel Kant, had never been more than six miles from their birthplace in the whole of their lives. There were representatives, too, from Roddy's secret life, one woman in particular whom I had known for some time without ever suspecting that she was an alcoholic. She was a successful cry for help and Roddy McMillan had been the one who had answered the call. She had trusted him and listened to him as one who understood because he had traversed the same dark landscape himself and survived. I had heard of his work with AA but only in a vague, generalised fashion. Now it seemed something infinitely greater, standing there with tears running down its face and its make-up ruined.

I had been asked to pay one of the tributes to the man and had sat up all night trying to put him into words; but the words refused to come, probably overpowered by the enormity of what they were confronting. Dawn was firmly established before the first line of a poem swam into my head and suddenly unblocked my mind. I finished it quickly then discovered that every time I tried to read it, I broke down. There was just no way I was ever going to be able to read it in public without embarrassing everybody. In the end, I called Paul Young and asked him to read it on my behalf, which he agreed to do, and which he did superbly.

Then it was all over and we dispersed, leaving Roddy McMillan to his long loneliness and we had a feeling that we had all lost something and that we had all become poorer. The theatre had lost a great actor and a fine writer both in terms of his proven achievements but even more so of his potential. We went home, remembering poems he had written and songs he had sung, jokes he had cracked and fights he had fought. And the rain poured down on our terrible knowledge that we would never see his like again.

Two days later, we went back down to the cottage in Galloway and at that spot, just outside Balmaclellan, I noticed that the do-it-yourself sign that bore the word "Torwatletie" was no longer there. I have looked for it many times since but it remains obstinately missing. The thought has occurred to me that perhaps it never was there and that perhaps there was never even any reason for it to be there. This led me to consult the relevant Ordnance Survey map, Sheet 73, New Galloway. Sure enough, you will find Torwatletie there with an untarred road leading to it. But the pathetic roadside sign has vanished. No doubt there is some perfectly ordinary and logical reason for this but if there is not, I would prefer not to know. I am not sure I could handle that.

They're no' supposed to smell, Missus

GLESCA OOT FOR A WALK

Eddie Boyd

He wis wan o' them and A' o' them
The crooked an' the crock
the big fat wumman wi' the wee thin block
the hard man, struttin' wi' his gamecock walk,
Kevin Barry an' Boyne Watter
(Hi McMillan, gie's yer patter!)
When ye saw him, ye saw Glesca
Oot for a walk.

The Devil took him up a hill,
showed London, spread oot flat,
an' said, "You gotta come down here
Man! This is where it's at."

"Bye, Superman!"

You'll make a killing here, old boy,
A killing? Nay, a slaughter.
Fancy a ten-bedroomed house
down in Virginia Water?
And, in every second bedroom
A redundant Earl's daughter?
I promise you, you'll soon forget
you ever had a poor day;
and Scotland will be a sometime thing
say once ayear–on Ne'erday.

He shook his heid: "Whit wad Ah need
Wi a' that dreary schlock?"
Then set off up the Great North Road
Glesca, oot for a walk.

O he wis wan o' them an' a' o' them
the folk in urban shock;
the big fat wumman wi' the wee thin block
the hard man struttin' wi' his gamecock walk
John Maclean and Benny Lynch
Folk who never gave an inch.
When ye saw him ye saw Glesca
oot for a Walk.

So farewell, Para Handy,
farewell Vital Spark;
and Daniel Pike has walked away
into that final dark.
The time has come for grieving,
the time is past for talk
Farewell Glesca,
oot for a walk.

THE GLASGOW CHARACTER

General Wolfe

THE MEN HERE are civil, designing and treacherous, with their immediate interests always in view. They pursue trade with warmth, and a necessary mercantile spirit, arising from the baseness of their other qualifications. The women are coarse, bold and cunning; forever inquiring after men's circumstances; they make that the standard of their good breeding. You may imagine it would not be difficult for me to be pretty well received here, if I took pains, having some of the advantages necessary to recommend me to their favour. But . . .

The Book Of Glasgow Anecdote

The stuff that dreams are made on

HOW I GOT GOUT IN GLASGOW

Hamish Imlach

MY FIRST WORDS on seeing the smoking tenements and factories of Glasgow as I arrived by train from London in July 1953, were "My God they must have suffered terribly during the war!" I was arriving "home", just into my teens after a fairly sheltered life in India and Australia, where I was made to wear a kilt on Sundays, and had imagined Scotland as a mysterious place of haunted castles and, of course, bagpipes, glens, bens, monsters and Granny's hielan' hames. The stark reality of a city that seemed to be still smouldering and blackened eight years after the war had ended, appalled me more than the filth and squalor of Calcutta, where I was born, had ever done.

Where did they put the old Grand Hotel when they turned Charing Cross into an abyss?

Thirty years later I find myself proudly showing off our beautiful sandstone tenements, the Kelvingrove Art Gallery and so on to visitors from overseas (or England and Edinburgh) and lamenting the disappearance of the countless buildings that had survived the war, only to be blitzed and bulldozed by bampot bureaucrats. I regale them with nostalgic tales of our trams, oor wee subway and the thrills and tribulations of illicit romances up closes and doon dunnies. I even went through a period when I would insist on taking apprehensive parties of Americans and Continentals to places like the Saracen Head and Paddy's Market. Love us or leave us. I found the ones who are still friends are the few who genuinely enjoyed themselves. A still test that—I'm sure a lot of Glaswegians would not pass it themselves.

I can't avoid the cliché of saying it was the people of Glasgow who opened my eyes and moulded my new attitude to the city, and, to me, people in Glasgow means pubs in Glasgow. Places where you couldn't remain a stranger for long. Camaraderie and chat would involve everyone present, with the topics ranging from football or fornication to philosophy or politics, and stoatin' one-liners like the old worthy looking out of the pub window at the pissing rain and remarking, "Aye, even Gene Kelly wouldnae go oot in that!"

Any trace of pomposity or pretension was pilloried. Pseuds and phonies were ignored or dismissed with devastating put-downs. I remember a young student dogmatically airing his views, and solutions to the state of the world, the nuclear threat, theology and the universe. A punter sitting nearby waited till he paused for breath and, putting his arm round his shoulder said solemnly, "Ach well son, as long as you've got your health." Bugger the playing fields of Eton, surviving in a Glasgow pub strengthened moral fibre and was a rare character builder.

I bought my first quarter gill in the Thornwood Bar on Dumbarton Road, which was then the last oasis before miles of dry areas to the North and West. A few years later I went into my first lounge bar in the newly opened Friend's Tavern, almost opposite. I felt uneasy. Subconciously I think I knew even then that this was the thin end of the wedge.

Even the cuddies in this town are fleein'

In 1960 I was a tiro performer, involved in running the Glasgow Folk Club (the first in Scotland) and we organised a concert for the great American folk singer, Cisco Houston, long-time friend and accompanist of the legendary Woody Guthrie. When I invited him out for a drink he staggered me by asking if I knew Betty's Bar and saying that he and Woody had spent many happy hours there during the war when they visited Glasgow as merchant seamen. We had a few drinks there together and his pleasure in revisiting the place was obvious. Now the new management are changing the image and barring the ladies who had been a feature of the place for nearly a 150 years. Ominous.

I'm becoming more and more apprehensive at the rash of twee wine bars and glaring plastic disco-pubs which make easy conversation impossible. How will future generations of Glaswegians be educated and taught manners? Juke boxes have been conquered with coins and superglue, but canned muzak and discos are more difficult. A Glasgow without pubs where you could get a quarter-gill hauf-and-haufpint in peace, with congenial company, is unthinkable. I comfort myself that the Thornwood Bar is still going strong and the new-fangled Friend's Tavern is long gone.

I'll wrap up with a quote from the late Jim Cairney, much-loved manager of Sandy Bell's, a pub in that other city, Edinburgh (I'm no bigot). When customers were complaining bitterly about a modest redecoration of the bar, Jim came out with the immortal words, "That's the trouble with this pub, it's full of bloody revolutionaries who want nothing to change." A thought-provoking line worthy of any Glasgow pub, and I can bestow no higher praise.

PS The title lied. I do suffer from gout, but it has no connection with the happy hours I spent imbibing in Glasgow.

Matt McGinn in flight

KNELL FOR BELL

Robert Dalglish, Esq.

HOW FLEETING is the life of man? Henry Bell—poor Henry Bell! whom we remember perfectly, and have often chatted with as the inventor and owner of the very first steamer that ever sailed on the River Clyde, named by him the *Comet*, of some few tons burthen, and not exceeding six horse-power—differing so much from the comet then careering in the skies, and alarming the world by its effulgence— but the very name given by him to his tiny steamer indicated somewhat of his inventive genius.

The last of a proud line

Henry Bell—poor, we say, and almost despised at the early period, though his name now can never die—was vexed and wearied almost to death by the rude jibes and jeers levelled at him while fitting up his little vessel to sail from Helensburgh to Greenock, and from Greenock to Dumbarton Castle, onwards to Bowling Bay and Glasgow.

He was literally ridiculed and laughed at. He was actually persecuted, as we have remarked for his original labours. We saw him seized as a prisoner by Mr Duncan Macfarlane, Messenger-at-Arms in Dumbarton, under a writ of caption for a debt of less than £20 for furnishings to his *Comet*. We hold the writ in our possession at this moment, and it is a curiosity.

. . . or the pool might catch fire

He had an only brother alive at that period, whose name was Thomas. The name of Henry was a sweet one, and nobody disliked it; but Tam or Thomas did not sound so pleasantly in the lips of others. He was generally addressed as "Tammas"; and Henry having erected the baths at Helensburgh, and placed a coach on the road between Helensburgh and Glasgow for the accommodation of passengers (which led him to think of the river accommodation), Tammas was installed by him as the guard or driver of that coach. It was a queer ricketty affair, travelling at the rate of some five miles per hour. But Tammas derived more money from that coach for a while than did his Brother Henry with his *Comet* Steamer.

One of his best patrons in that coach, and who joked with Henry about his *Comet*, was old Mr John Napier, who, next to James, was the first engineer, beyond all question, in Glasgow. He had, besides Camlachie, his small place of business in Howard Street, and old Mr John Napier had erected, or was then building a handsome cottage, as it was then thought to be, on the shores of Cardross. We remember very well of hearing, not once or twice, but often and again, old Mr John Napier, with Major-General Thomas Geils of Ardmore and others, discussing with Henry Bell his original plans about the *Comet*, while he himself would be developing them out with his pencil. How afterwards, yet then in our teens, we rejoiced when we beheld that wonderful steamer the *Comet* dashing up on her very first voyage against the wind and the waves to Glasgow!

We have preserved and retain in our possession at this day, one of the original passenger tickets of the *Comet*, representing the tiny boat as gliding past Dumbarton Castle, which ticket was presented to us by the amiable widow of Henry Bell. It is of the year 1811, and looks as fresh as yesterday.

Reminiscences of Glasgow

THE BLUE DOO

James Copland

There was wunst a wee doo,
An' this wee doo was blue,
It had got itsel' right in a mess.
Now it might be that you
Never heard of this doo,
Well ah'll tell ye for you'd never guess.

Well, this wee doo was seeck,
It had banjo'd its beak,
Jist wi' stabbin' a daud of stale breid.
When alang came a boy,
Jist a durrty wee boy,
Who had snotters an' beasts in his heid.

Said the wee boy—Aw jings!
Ah love a' things wi' wings!
An' he gave the wee doo a big cuddle,
Then he mendit its beak,
He jist gave it a tweak,
Then he saftened its breid in a puddle.

Well, the doo gulped the breid,
It wiz hunger—no' greed,
An' it said tae the boy—thanksalo',
For yir jist a wee pe',
An' ah'll never forge',
End the truth is it nevah forgot!

So youse people take heed,
Ayeways saften doo's breid,
An' never smack boys who have beasts in thir heid,
For ye might smack the boy
Who was good to the doo,
An' the next thing ye'll know is—
The doo might get you!

University and unsleeping sentinel

The Forth and Clyde

NO ESCAPE

Robert Dalglish, Esq.

A FEW EVENINGS before the evening of his execution, Wm. Clydesdale, the miserable murderer, was treated to a glass of porter by Mr John M'Gregor, long the humane governor of the prison—a powerful, strong-built man, who could carry Clydesdale with ease under his left arm. Clydesdale was then in a most exhausted state, and he relished the glass of porter exceedingly. The governor perceiving this, said "that in place of the bread and water allotted to him by his sentence, he (the governor) would bring him a bottle of porter the next time he visited him in his cell".

Clydesdale expressed his thanks. The bottle of porter was soon brought, as promised, by the jailor, and Clydesdale quaffed off the better part of it in a small tumbler brought for that purpose. Ere he was locked up for the night, he beseeched Mr M'Gregor, the jailor, to leave the bottle, with the rest of its contents, for his use during his few allotted hours. The humane jailor, with the approbation of his turnkeys, having no suspicion at all, at once granted this request. They parted with the prisoner heavily ironed for the night, and carefully locked the doors of his dismal iron cell. Outwardly there was no possibility for him to escape; they therefore retired to their own apartments, and fell asleep.

Scandal, shock, horror

When they awakened on the following morning, and went, confident as usual, to the condemned cell, they were horrified to find the prisoner on the floor, bleeding to death. They discovered, that he had broken the bottle which contained the relished porter, and lacerated his throat and arms with it, that he might die in this manner, rather than go to the scaffold or to the anatomy rooms of Dr Jeffrey in the College.

This, of course, placed the respected jailor in an agony of consternation; and not only him and his turnkeys, but the whole Magistrates of the city, because the sentence of the Court was that the prisoner should only be fed "on bread and water", whereas the jailor, for whom the Magistrates were responsible, had allowed him this bottle of porter!

What was now to be done? To stanch the bleeding wounds and preserve—strange to say!—the life of the wretched prisoner for the scaffold, to undergo also his after doom, Dr Corkindale, the surgeon of the prison, with several of the most eminent surgeons and physicians of the city, were called quickly to the Tolbooth to dress the bleeding wounds of this murderer, inflicted by his own hands, and they succeeded.

The hour of his execution at last arrived, and the scaffold was surrounded and guarded by the 40th Regiment of Foot, and a strong detachment of the First Dragoon Guards, then stationed in Glasgow. The crowd was immense. We shall say nothing more about it, except this, that Thomas Young, the Glasgow hangman, most kindly and affectionately, to all outward appearances, at least, shook the poor prisoner cordially by the hand; and the prisoner—in his white gloves, and white night-cap drawn over his ears, and the fatal noose carefully adjusted round his neck—turned round and shook Thomas, apparently most cordially, in return; and then the fatal *jerk* ensued, which can never be heard again under the same circumstances.

Reminiscences of Glasgow

HENGLER'S GRAND CIRQUE

Jack House

GLASGOW HAS never been the same to me since the disappearance of Hengler's Circus in Sauchiehall Street. It was the first live entertainment I ever saw because it was even before I saw my first pantomime. And I was there every year until Mr Hengler gave up, somewhere around 1925 -26. I even saw the show one New Year's morning, when the first of four performances that day started at 10 a.m. Of course, I didn't drink then.

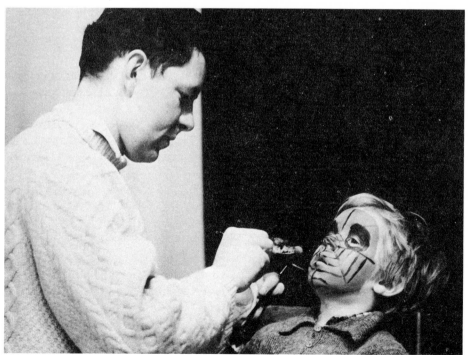

An old tribal custom

Words . . .

Hengler's had appeared on one or two sites in Glasgow before it settled down in the Sauchiehall Street building. It stood just below the School of Art and the place is now occupied by the ABC One and Two cinemas.

Although I have been to the circus in New York, Moscow, Paris, London, Belfast and Guadalajara, Mexico, not one has had the same effect on me as Hengler's Grand Cirque had. The point, of course, was that all Glaswegians considered it as "our" circus, conveniently ignoring the fact that Hengler's played the summer at the Tower Circus in Blackpool.

I've often wondered how Doodles got on at Blackpool. Doodles, one of the best clowns I've ever seen, was actually William McAllister of Glasgow, a real wee bachle and a fine acrobat as well as being acutely funny. I never saw him at Blackpool so I don't know what he did about his accent there. Glasgow people didn't go to Blackpool then.

To be technical, Doodles wasn't really a clown but an *Auguste*. The clown is the chap with the white face and pointed hat. The auguste is the tramp character and fool of the show. Doodles was a tramp character all right and, just to make confusion worse confounded, he had an auguste who was also a tramp character. In fact, the act was billed as "Doodles and Auguste".

Unlike some circus clowns today Doodles didn't make one or two appearances in the show. He was in the ring almost all the time and his bouts of barney with the Ringmaster, a fine figure of a man with a magnificent moustache, were among the highlights of Hengler's.

At Haghill School in Dennistoun you were nobody if you hadn't been to
Hengler's. I remember one year when, for some reason, my father postponed the
annual visit to February. By that time, of course, practically every boy in my class
had been to Hengler's. In order not to lose face, I pretended I had been to the
circus too. All was well until a big argument arose about the final Water Scene. I'll
come to the stupendous Water Scene later, but it could be described as a
melodrama with spectacular effects that you couldn't see anywhere else.

This year it was a Cowboys and Indians affair and the argument at Haghill
was whether, at one point in the action, the Indians attacked up a ladder or a stair.
Since I had said I'd seen the show, some of the boys appealed to me for my
adjudication. The boy who was foremost for the ladder was friend of mine so I
took his side and averred firmly that the Indians went up a ladder. Some weeks
later my father took us to Hengler's and there, before my very eyes, I saw the
Indians attack up a stair. It was then that I decided never to tell lies again and
every time I'm tempted to tell a whopper, I think of Hengler's and try to desist.

Hengler's had all the best-known circus acts and you watched the acrobats, the
jugglers (Doodles could juggle too), the elephants, the horses, the fire-eaters, the
Strongest Man in the World, the lions, and enjoyed the show immensely. But
then the finale of the circus part of the show took place and the ring-men entered
to remove the various carpets and effects. Doodles helped, of course, and ended by
being carried off inside a carpet. Then a hush fell. Every eye was on the floor of
the ring. Suddenly water would come gushing up through the holes in the floor

. . . and music

and the ring itself would slowly descend, leaving a lake in its place.

Curtains at the back of the lake would part and reveal the opening scene of the play. The actors got through the preliminaries as quickly as possible. They knew the audience was waiting for the thrills. Sure enough, when the curtains reopened we were looking across the lake at a great mountain towering to the very top of the circus.

The plot didn't really matter but on this occasion a gallant cowboy was defending his girl friend from the infamous intentions of an evil rancher. Eventually upon the mountain top the gallant cowboy and the girl were facing the evil rancher who was proposing to shoot the cowboy and abduct the girl. It didn't strike us at the time that the cowboy must have mislaid his gun. Just as the evil rancher raised his six-shooter there was a peal of thunder (and though Hengler's advertised that rifle shots were no louder than the crack of a whip, they fairly went to town on the thunder). Then came a flash of lightning. It hit the top of the mountain and split it in two, with the cowboy and his girl on one side of the gap and the evil rancher on the other.

They lost on the swings. High life on Glasgow Green

There must have been a lake on the other side as well as ours for now water came rushing through the gap and soon an immense waterfall came thundering down into the lake in front of us.

And then, for no apparent reason, the Indians came in canoes and, one after the other, went over the waterfall and dived into our lake. None of the Indians was killed. They all swam successfully to the shore. The lights went up. Hengler's band played "God save the King" and, somewhat shattered, we tottered out of the circus.

If this description sounds a trifle incoherent, it's a piece of dazzling realism compared with the average Hengler's spectacle script. Sometimes I felt there hadn't been a script at all and the actors just made it up as they went along. They must have known as well as we did that we weren't there for Shakespeare. It was the ring of bright water that had us there every year.

Alas, Mr Hengler gave up. I don't remember why. Realising that a winter circus was absolutely necessary, Glasgow Corporation started their civic circus (no, not the one in George Square) in the Kelvin Hall. So I still go to the circus every year and the standard is very high. But there's no water spectacle and there's no Doodles.

What happened to Doodles? He was a friend of the ageing Sir Harry Lauder and the up-and-coming Tommy Lorne. Presumably he went on appearing in circuses until he had to retire. He did come back to Glasgow and spent his declining years here. And declining is the operative word. When William McAllister died he left no money and his Doodles "props" were sold for just over £4. Laugh, Clown, Laugh!

Service with a smile

SEEN FROM FRANCE

Christian Civardi

AND YET . . . and yet, Glasgow is a pearl among cities. A rose rises from the muck. A town whose people know themselves, make themselves known, question, discuss, debate, sing, rejoice, weep and vibrate together. A town which has fashioned an authentic urban folklore, a popular civic culture. Whether of Saxon or Celtic origin, Italian, Polish, Lithuanian or Pakistani, Catholic, Protestant or Muslim, proletarian or bourgeois, boozer or teetotal, male or female, the Glaswegian—that is to say one Scot in three—is easier to define than the Parisian, the Londoner or the Edimbourgeois, no doubt thanks to the great homogeneity of the conditions of life, habitation and work.

He (she) is—and this is what strikes you at once—always in motion; pedestrians who can't wait their turn to cross, strangers who can't see you hesitate at a crossing without coming to offer you directions, talkers who can't talk without dragging frenziedly on a cigarette, or making the sign of the head, the famous Glasgow twitch, also found in Ireland, and punctuating the talk with the guttural "och aye" and "ach no" as if they needed to assure themselves that their bodies are still working, as if the briefest moment of immobility would open before them the awful abyss of existential despair.

Crossing the canyon

Jamieson Clark and Big John Rannie

He is simple, direct and without guile. He distrusts affectation and the smart Alecs who put on airs, the poseurs who affect an Oxford accent and dress themselves at Burton's. Combining the anarchic tendencies of the Gaels with the acid critical spirit of the Lowlanders, capable of deflating the mightiest pretension, the Glaswegian is thoroughly egalitarian. "A man's a man for a' that" is the Burns line he quotes most.

Don't expect him to give you a deferential "sir". Dress yourself like a lord, nothing will stop the Glaswegian from asking you in the immutable terms, "Have ye got the time oan ye, Jimmy?" In Glasgow, they call every man Jimmy or Mac, and every woman Hen. In all logic, he votes Left (he detests the élitism of the Tories, and their Edinburgh-London manners), but is implacably opposed to economic, social and cultural changes that shock his working-class conservatism.

It is a hugely sentimental city. Glasgow is one of the rare towns (with Fellinicittà) where you could cry in the street without fear of ridicule, and with the near-certainty that somebody would come to console you. They love crowds and great collective emotions because, like Fellini's citizens, the Glaswegian is gregarious. Doubtless conditioned by the anthills where he works and the burrows where he lives, he can't conceive of leisure except in the company of crowds. Nothing seems to put him off so much as the intimacy of a small room; perhaps it is as much for that reason as from puritanism that Glasgow, a seaport, has hardly any cabarets or nightclubs. In compensation, the town possesses the second biggest football ground in the world, Hampden Park, and the biggest cinema in

Europe. In relation to its population, it has held or holds the British records for the number of music-halls, theatres, dance-halls, cafés, pleasure boats and bingo-halls.

(Translated from Ecosse *by Christian Civardi, in the collections microcosme*
Petite Planet, 1980.)

FRIENDS AT COURT

Joe Beltrami

I COUNSEL YOU—do not be misled by the name. If you are born and brought up in Glasgow, you're a Glaswegian, and that's that.

I spent my first twenty-five years in the vortex of Glasgow, the famous "Briggait", within a good drop kick of our recently refurbished High Court building in Saltmarket. Many a football match took place on waste ground there (now a sedate car park) with the inevitable tanner ba', and an indeterminate number of players.

The number of players in these games, of course, was never restricted, nor was any quarter given or sought. Even the rules were flexible. Bernard Corrigan, John McGlone, John Ramage and myself—to name only a few—played regularly until either utter exhaustion or darkness brought proceedings to an end.

I still remember the galling experience of being lined up before the two "captains" and, one by one, being selected for the teams. The longer it took to be selected, the more you realised that there was room for improvement in your skills. If you were one of the last, no-one bothered if you were left out—you were expendable.

In addition, you had to be able to fight . . . I remember, in 1939, the year the Second World War broke out, being sent to the local school, St Andrew's, in Ropework Lane, off Clyde Street. On my very first day there I was confronted by Francie McKenna, who was, apparently, by his own admission, the best fighter in the school. There I was, minding my own business, when I was challenged by Francie, who had clearly decided that he must maintain his reputation and honour at my expense. I managed to settle the matter amicably and without violence. I even compounded matters by making Francie my very best friend. Since that moment I have always believed in tactics—later, I was to become a lawyer and to win many a case by first assessing the strength of the opposition and organising a tactical approach.

Those were good days in the "Briggait". Things like baths,showers and hot water were considered cissy and unnecessary—in any event, these luxuries were not common amenities in the neighbourhood in which I grew up.

I was only seven years old when the last World War was declared. I remember seeing a newspaper bill at the junction of Glassford Street and Trongate—"War Declared". I ran to my home at 132 Bridgegate and quickly put on my cowboy outfit and, duly armed with a six-shooter and a toy rifle, I proceeded to patrol the full extent of my block. I still recall my disappointment when nothing happened and the populace seemed to be going about their normal daily business. Not a German in sight!

It was just over 34 years ago when I got on a tramcar in Stockwell Street and rode with it to Gilmorehill, to matriculate as a student at Glasgow University. When I got on the tram I was going to be a schoolteacher. When I got off I had decided to become a lawyer. The decision to take up law rather than teaching was made in the space of four tram-stops, between Charing Cross and Gilmorehill. That change of mind had been brought about by a schoolfriend, Kevin Purcell, who boarded the tram at Charing Cross and sat beside me. He told me that he was going to matriculate in law—because he had just heard that the Legal Aid (Scotland) Act of 1949 had been passed. And, in his opinion, law was the profession to enter.

I mulled this over in the course of four tram stages—and duly matriculated in the Faculty of Law. In June 1953 I graduated Bachelor of Law, when I was 21, and entered the legal world. . . .

As a lawyer, Glasgow was to be my oyster. I was to find that there was, of course, a very serious and sometimes grim side to my work in the law courts—but, being Glasgow, there was to be a lot of humour, too.

Glasgow Sheriff Court is among the busiest in Europe and the city has always produced its share of good lawyers. But a certain protocol obtains—and many of the principal participants in High Court cases come from Edinburgh and the East.

These wise men—judges, prosecutors and defence counsel—make their frequent pilgrimages to the West, apparently to regulate our senior courts and to ensure that matters do not get out of hand. Alas, this has led to some quaint misunderstandings, especially when Glasgow's own brand of humour surfaces, or the incomers are scuppered by the vernacular, 'an 'at.

There was a case of serious assault being tried, during which the prosecutor asked the victim how he received his injuries. This worthy replied, "Him there in the dock, between the two polis, smashed his way intae ma hoose, ran to the mantelpiece, picked up ma clock (pronounced, of course, 'cloak') and hit me o'er the heid wi' it". The prosecutor was seen to sigh, scratch his wig and pause. Clearly perplexed, he inquired, "Do you normally keep a cloak draped over your fireplace?"

Another time, there was a case of the unfortunate woman who had been savagely and brutally raped. Struggling for something to say to the victim, Defence Counsel broke his silence by observing, "I take it this was a rare occurrence for you?" Quick as a flash came the outraged rejoinder—"You might think it was rerr—Ah thought it was bloody terrible."

Not all the humour stems from our learned friends from the East, of course. For example, there was the Judge who came to be known to most of us as "The Messiah". This judge was noted for his savage sentences and was feared by all accused persons. Many "bailers" who turned up at Glasgow Sheriff Court to find that their cases were to come before this man contrived not to find their way to his court. He acquired his nickname when three accused, well-known for their violent disposition, were due to appear before him. They made their way up the eighteen steps that led from the cells, in the bowels of the High Court, to the dock of the courtroom. As the first one's head emerged at dock level his eyes lighted on the scowling but resplendent figure on the Bench. The accused suddenly turned round and cried to the others, "Jesus Christ, It's him!" Henceforth the judge was known among the fraternity as "The Messiah".

Once, an accused came before "The Messiah", charged with reckless driving and driving without insurance. The accused, who had no lawyer to represent him, was arrogant and had, on two previous occasions, failed to turn up at court. A warrant had been taken out for his arrest and he was duly escorted into court. It turned out that he had been particularly cheeky to the police at the time of his arrest, and he was cheeky and over-confident as he conducted his own defence. After being found guilty he was asked if he wished to say anything with regard to the possibility of disqualification from driving. In a somewhat off-hand manner he stated that if he lost his licence he would lose his job and become a liability on

City of Angels

the State. He told "The Messiah", "You cannot, in all conscience, disqualify me from driving".

There followed several exchanges between the Bench and the accused, with the latter losing much of his self-assurance. Finally, almost reduced to tears, the accused pleaded, "Please don't disqualify me from driving". "The Messiah", still upset at the man's whole conduct throughout the case, looked at the accused in the way that only he can do and said, "Get f---ing lost".

Those in Court were shocked—indeed, positively aghast—had the learned Sheriff, to use the vernacular, "flipped his lid"? Quick as a flash, sharp as a tack and always a move ahead, "The Messiah" leaned towards the Procurator Fiscal and said, "Was not that the reply the accused made when he was cautioned and charged with the offences?" The Fiscal, never slow off the mark himself in these matters, was quick to agree that the accused's reply had, indeed, been in those terms!

On the day that "The Messiah" sentenced an accused to 30 days' imprisonment (he must have been in a particularly good mood) the recipient of this punishment was heard to mutter, "Good, I'll do that standing on ma heid." Again as quick as a flash, "The Messiah" retorted, "Well, you can just do another 30 days to help you back on your feet!"

It wasn't yesterday when I represented "Big Frank" on a charge of murdering "Big Tam" in the Gorbals. No lesser weapon than a large sword had been used to smite Tam who had many convictions, had been a money-lender, extortionist and was an extremely disreputable character. Hence, even criminals detested Tam for his bullying activities. My client Frank was six feet two inches and was built in proportion. He vehemently denied the charge right from the start; the two witnesses who had picked him out at an Identification Parade were "hopelessly mistaken". The mere thought that Frank would need little short of a claymore to kill Tam in the first place, was enough to infuriate my client.

The Trial was fought vigorously, but, regrettably, the Jury found him guilty of murder and he received the mandatory life sentence. I spoke to Counsel and said that we would have to see him in the cells at once. Counsel was none too happy about this daunting prospect and neither was I, to be honest. In trepidation, we went downstairs and I arranged for a number of policemen to be placed at strategic points around the cell area—just in case. I vividly recall my feeling of great unease as the cell door was opened and my sheer desperation in trying to invent possible excuses for the verdict. Big Frank emerged and declared (to our immense satisfaction and relief), "Killing that bastard—it was worth it!" Come to think of it, that was the first time I saw him smile.

Glasgow identification parades could be that little bit different too . . . I well remember one particular incident regarding a nasty rape case. The witness to the rape walked along the line of six men, stopped at my client, number five, and, without warning, delivered a perfect right cross to his unprotected jaw and felled him. It was just like the time that Jackie Paterson knocked out Peter Kane in all of 67 seconds to win the World Flyweight title at Hampden Park. After felling my client the witness said, somewhat unnecessarily I thought, "That's him".

Another identification case involved an Irish labourer, who was also charged with rape. The police went out of their way to ensure fair play. The Irishman was six foot tall and the police found five other stand-ins of equal height. They also matched hairstyles, complexions—and even made sure that they all wore black "welly" boots. I was very pleased with the composition of the parade. The complainer was duly summoned and a deathly hush ensued as the victim, still shocked, was helped down the line of men. As we all wondered what she would do, my client suddenly stepped forward, pointed to the woman and shouted at the top of his voice, "Sure, that's her, that's the very wumman." As you can imagine, emergency insanity proceedings were invoked!

Among other lighter moments I can recall from days in Court was the time that a particularly heated exchange developed between a Sheriff and the Fiscal over a plea I made for bail for my client. After almost ten minutes of quite vituperative confrontation in which both Sheriff and Fiscal were often speaking or shouting in unison, the Sheriff barked at the Fiscal, "Don't you dare interrupt me when I'm interrupting you!"

There are often priceless examples of the Glaswegian's famous flair for repartee. Such as the time Sheriff Langmuir was addressing three youths charged with breach of the peace. One of them had an inordinate mass of hair. They had all pled guilty to the charge. The Sheriff sentenced his two companions to a fine of £10 and then said—rather harshly—to the third, hairy accused, "Look at you—you are like a relic from the time of Charles the First!" Quick as a flash the accused countered, "I hope you aren't considering the same sentence".

Looking back, it has to be said that despite the fairly primitive living conditions in downtown Glasgow there were no drug or glue-sniffing problems, no mention of heroin or cocaine or cannabis, let alone using such substances.

Regrets? Yes, I lament the passing of the city's boxing legends. I enjoyed watching some of the "greats"—like Jackie Paterson and Peter Keenan. What has happened to the fight scene now?

But I still treasure the many good things of this city of my birth. Glasgow, and the warmth and humour of its people, will always be close to my heart—no mean city, indeed.

LAW AND ORDER

Robert Dalglish, Esq.

IN CONSEQUENCE of the riotous assembly and assault on the house of Mr Dreghorn, a number of persons were apprehended, but of these we need only give the names of Richard Campbell, weaver; John Macmillan, painter; John Campbell, shoemaker; James Brown, packman; and John Munro, weaver, because these were publicly brought to trial before the Circuit Court of Justiciary in the month of April, 1822.

The fact of their complicity and guilt was clearly established. The case against Campbell was more flagrant than that of the others, inasmuch as he had been at one time an old police officer; and instead of aiding the police on this occasion, he had incited the mob to repulse them, and to stone the Magistrates. The jury, without leaving the box, unanimously found the whole of them to be guilty. They were sentenced to be transported beyond seas for the space of fourteen years; but in addition, Campbell, as being the ringleader, was adjudged to be scourged through the city, by the hangman, on the 8th day of May following.

Accordingly, on that memorable 8th day of May, 1822, at 12 o'clock, a strong detachment of the 4th Dragoon Guards paraded in front of the Jail, and at the same time a strong party of police and civil officers attended, under the direction of Mr James Hardie, the Superintendent of Police. Soon afterwards, the convicted culprit was brought out of the Jail by the north door, and bound to a cart which was in waiting. Parties of the Dragoons were placed in front and rear to keep off the crowd; and when all was ready, the cavalcade moved round to the area on the south side of the Jail, where the culprit's back was laid bare by the hangman, who gave him his first twenty lashes with a formidable "cat o' nine tails", always so called.

The like punishment was repeated at the foot of the Stockwell, and also at the head of the Stockwell; but the last twenty lashes, making eighty in all, were given

Everything brand new

by Thomas Young, the hangman, at the crowded Cross of Glasgow—the prisoner groaning and lamenting his fate; but this terrible example had the most salutory effect—it taught the mob that there was a power over them after all.

Of Thomas Young, that old Glasgow hangman, we may here add a very few words. He was, as we very well remember, a tall, lean, lank man, apparently of good disposition. Since his exit from Glasgow, our city authorities have wisely shut up the old hangman's house, and beckon Mr Calcraft from London; and we join in the wish that the seldomer he is seen here the better. His absence, indeed, is significant of good company; but the last finisher of the law is entitled to every respect in all proper cases; and to this surely some of our readers will say, Amen!

Reminiscences of Glasgow

Crepuscule

COD LIVER OIL AND THE ORANGE JUICE

Carl MacDougall

THIS SONG WAS originally a spontaneous parody on a solemn religious ditty about three wise men from the east, first heard by the author in a Glasgow tavern.

MacDougall couldn't believe anybody could be so solemn. The original song has vanished without trace, buried under the weight of the parody.

It was oot o the east there came a wee hard man
Aw haw, aa the wey fae Brigton
(*Chorus*)
Ah-ha, Glory Hallelujah
Cod liver oil and the orange juice

He went intae a pub and he came oot paraletic
Aw haw, the VP and the cider

Does this bus go tae the Denny-Palais
Aw haw, Ah'm lookin' for a lumber

In the Palais he met Hairy Mary
Aw haw, the flooer o the Calton

He says tae her, Tell me hen are ye dancin'?
Aw naw, it's jist the wey Ah'm staunin

He says tae her, You're wan in a million
Aw haw, so's yer chances

Can Ah run ye hame Ah've goat a pair a saunies
Aw haw, you're helluva funny

Up the back close and doon the dunny
Aw naw, it wisnae fur the first time

Aha ha, it wisnae fur the last time
Cod liver oil and the orange juice

Her maw came oot tae go tae the cludgy
Aw haw, he buggered off sharpish

She tried tae find the hard man, he's jined the Foreign Legion
Aw haw, Sahara and the camels

So Hairy Mary had a little baby
Aw haw, its faither's in the army

Ah-ha, Glory Hallelujah
The cod liver oil and the orange juice.

. . . and was then remembered at Rotten Row

BY NO MEANS MEAN

Bashir Ahmed Maan

I HAVE NOW lived in Glasgow for thirty-one years. This great city has a bad reputation, but is in fact an extrovert, tolerant and warm-hearted place.

Even the notorious inebriates in this city are courteous and friendly. They may be in an unsteady state themselves, but I have seen many of them offering help and showing concern to the strangers they come across in their usual manner of saying, "You all right, Jimmy?"

The drunks of this city, like others, do fight among themselves. But unlike others they make up as soon as the influence wears off. I lived in Townhead for about ten years in a tenement. Every Friday and Saturday night, just after midnight, the noise of shouting and abuse grew in the house next door and developed into a brawl. Then the door would burst open and the punching, kicking, cursing and shouting would continue in the common close till the "visitors" were thrown out onto the street. The door would then be shut with a

Let us haste to Kelvingrove

loud bangs and the shouting and cursing would stop. The bruises and wounds would be attended to by the womenfolk and when everything had returned to normal we would all go to sleep.

About five or six o'clock in the morning one would be awakened by a loud knocking at the door of the same house. The door would eventually open and one would hear apologies being offered on both sides for the last night's violence, and

A wee birl round the Burrell

peace would be made again without any mediation and without any fuss. This I think is a rare and unique quality of Glaswegians. Once the dust settles down they hasten to apologise and make peace without any qualms or reservations. They are not vindictive. They forget and forgive.

I have also found Glaswegians very broadminded. I was adopted as a Labour candidate for the Kingston Ward in the municipal elections of 1970. The sitting councillor at that time was a courteous, hard-working Tory gentleman. There were two other candidates representing the Scottish National and Communist Parties. Altogether we were four candidates and I was the odd man out, being of a different race, different religion and most obviously of different colour. My chances of winning the election, therefore, were rated as nil. Even my election agent, the veteran Harry Selby, who became an MP a few years later, told me in so many words that I had no chance.

I, however, having then lived in Glasgow for seventeen years and having experienced the broadmindedness and the friendliness of the people of Glasgow, had a different opinion. I was confident in my mind that if I put the required effort into the election campaign and tried to reach and meet as many electors as possible they would not reject me because of my race or colour. So I started my election campaign early and with the help of my friends and supporters introduced myself to a majority of the electors before polling day. I got a very good reception from the people of Kingston, at their doorsteps and in the streets, whenever and wherever I met them. The canvass returns started to look promising. On polling day we had a very good team and I went round every street many times with a loudspeaker exhorting the electors to come out and vote for me. At one of the polling stations early in the morning I met the agent of one of the other candidates. He remarked sarcastically that I had an advantage of 105 votes over them. I did not comprehend what he was saying and asked him what he meant. He said that there were 105 coloured voters in the ward, meaning perhaps that only 105 electors of Asian origin would vote for me. I retorted that in that case he had an advantage of 10,000 votes over me (as there were about 10,000 local voters on the roll) and suggested that we had better wait for the judgment of the electors when the votes were counted that night.

After the polling stations were closed, I went to the Kelvin Hall for the count. During the count the heap of the counted bundles of ballot papers for me started to become bigger and bigger and it became obvious that I was going to win. Soon after, when all the checking and other formalities were over, the returning officer declared the result. I had won with an absolute majority, obtaining 55 per cent of the total vote cast. The three other candidates, who were all Scottish and white, shared 45 per cent of the votes amongst them.

Ex-Provost and Bailie–Gray and Maan

The people of Kingston had conquered racial and colour prejudice and I and Labour had won this elusive seat which had been Tory for many years. The people of Glasgow had treated a man for what he stood for and not for what and who he was.

Islam on the Clyde–the new Mosque

Glasgow's friendliness has become proverbial amongst the Asian people in particular and the coloured communities in general. It is a common saying among them that once you have lived in Glasgow you cannot live anywhere else. Those who move away from Glasgow can seldom settle in a new place and nine out of ten come back.

Only in Glasgow will you find a complete stranger (a local person) greeting you or just nodding his or her head accompanied by "Hi Ya", "Good Morning" or some remark about the weather and a broad smile, just to be courteous and friendly. I remember once being reprimanded very severely by an old lady for ignoring her while I was going down and she was coming up a flight of stairs. She called me back and told me in no uncertain terms that it was ignorant and very rude of me to pass somebody without speaking, or at least smiling at them. She had greeted me with a smile and I, due to my shyness, as I had just come to this country, moved away without any response. So she gave me a piece of her mind, and that reprimand certainly did me a lot of good.

My first impression of the people of Glasgow was one I would never forget. I came to Glasgow in February 1953. The next day I went out on my own in the afternoon to look around. When it started to get dark I headed back to my lodgings, but to my horror I realised that I had lost my way. After trying my best, without any success, to get my bearings, very reluctantly and very apprehensively I approached an old man standing at a street corner and asked him the way to Hospital Street,

Gorbals, where I was staying. The old man, who was about seventy years of age, five-feet-sixish, rather lean, well wrapped up and wearing a bunnet, reacted in a very friendly manner and tried to give me directions. However, being unused to the Glasgow accent I was totally unable to comprehend what the gentleman was trying to tell me and felt even further confused.

It was nearly fifteen minutes before it became obvious to him that he was not getting through to me. In desperation, but with a broad smile, he grabbed my hand and gestured me to follow him, muttering, if I can recollect and interpret correctly, something like "Ach away, ah canny leave you staunin here or wandering aboot the streets aw night in this cauld weather." We must have walked for about twenty or twenty-five minutes when we came to Gorbals Cross which I recognised. I tried to tell the man that I knew my way home from there. But he kept walking in front of me beckoning me on till we reached my tenement close. He pointed at the number plate in the close and said, "Aw right, son?"

Overwhelmed with relief and gratitude towards this noble citizen of Glasgow, I was unable to utter a word and just nodded my head in affirmation. At this he left and I never saw him after that. Perhaps he is dead, but the memory of his generous deed lives on in my mind. This was my first encounter with an anonymous resident of the city which was to become my adopted home. It epitomises the nature of the people of Glasgow.

Glasgow unfortunately is also the most misunderstood and misrepresented place in this country. Nearly everybody who lives in this great city finds it friendly and full of life. Ironically, some of those sons of Glasgow to whom Glasgow has been very generous and who have consequently become famous, denigrate their city and run it down at every opportunity they get. One would assume that coming from Glasgow these well-known people would show some loyalty, but for some inexplicable reasons they feel compelled to demean Glasgow. Such people, more than anything else, are perpetually blackening this great city and giving it a bad name by their cheap jokes, exaggerated talk and speeches, one-sided broadcasts or sensationalist articles.

Therefore, I don't think there is any great need to sell Glasgow as is often suggested by those concerned about the reputation of the city; what is needed is a little care and a little restraint on the part of famous Glaswegians not to sell Glasgow down the river. If that can be achieved, I don't see any reason why Glasgow should not be able to shake off its bad image in the near future.

Glasgow has its problems. But these are not any different from, or any worse than, the problems of any other big city. As a matter of fact, Glasgow has a far better record than is commonly believed. It is a fact that the number of muggings, or assaults and robberies, is lower here than in many other cities; the passengers travelling on buses and underground are safer than anywhere else. It has been noted that there has been a steady decrease in accidents and injuries to passengers on Glasgow buses. Pornography and vice, which are giving headaches to police forces in other parts of this country, depraving and corrupting the citizens, are not a problem of any significance in Glasgow. The tolerance and bigheartedness of the people of Glasgow also becomes more obvious when one looks at its exemplary race relations. Glasgow football fans may be boisterous and unkempt, but they have never been bad enough to rip apart British Rail carriages as has happened in other parts of the country. So one can go on . . . and on . . . to shatter the myths and falsehoods.

The critics regrettably fail to look at the brighter and more attractive facets of Glasgow. They don't bother to mention that Glasgow is noted for an abundance of beautiful parks and gardens (the word "Glasgow" means "dear green place"), pleasant and refreshing river walkways, a unique fossil grove, wonderful art galleries and museums, world famous universities, well-stocked and comprehensive libraries, comfortable cinemas and good theatres, a very advanced urban highway system, convenient, extensive and competitive shopping precincts, excellent golf courses, many cricket, hockey and football grounds, and various other sporting facilities, to make the lives of the citizens easier and more enjoyable.

Glasgow is so ideally situated that half an hour's drive can take a sea-lover to sandy beaches on the coast; a lover of nature to captivating lochs and majestic highlands; a student of history to magnificent monuments steeped in the past. So! Glasgow is not a Mean City to live in and all those who have the privilege of living in it, I am sure, are proud of its greatness.

FOUR GLASGOW SUBWAY POEMS

Edwin Morgan

THE HISTORY of these works is almost as entertaining as the poems themselves. Eddie Morgan was one of four writers invited to provide words for posters in Glasgow's modernised underground system, known locally as the Clockwork Orange. The Morgan works were judged unsuitable by the Transport Executive, whose spokesman said, among other things, "There is no guard on Underground trains, no smoking or drinking is allowed, and the Subway Piranhas, it was felt, was wide open for parody. We must take this opportunity to assure our passengers that there are no piranha fish in the Underground."

Glasgow Herald readers rushed to the poet's defence in letters to the editor, both in prose and poetry, though one at least declared that "nice pictures of Victorian Glasgow" would be more appropriate than the neither-rhyme-nor-reason "poems" quite rightly rejected. Anyway, they have been produced as posters, on sale from the National Book League, 15a Lynedoch Street, Glasgow.

THE SUBWAY BUDGIE

Spirit of the place,
mascot of the enterprise,
lurking in the tunnels,
flashing past windows
or riding on the roof,
perky yet shy,
talkative but elusive,
she's a ball of gold
like a light's reflection,
a chatterbox
you think you heard
but turn your paper
and shake your head
as the train gathers speed.
The guard is her friend
and drops a few crumbs.
She picks, pecks, turns,
a magic bird,
a clockwork orange.

THE SUBWAY GIRAFFE

The subway giraffe
keeps its head down.
It has a special joint
in its neck. Its mother
is known to have been friendly
with an excavator.
It feeds on old tickets,
a cold chip or two,
makes do with cigarette-ends
but shivers with pleasure
at a scatter of rings
torn off from cans,
smacks its lips
as the metal rattles
down to its stomach.
The neighbours nod wisely:
'Favours his da.'

A master at work. Marzaroli protecting his eyes from the glare

THE SUBWAY CAT

The subway cat
just loves to sing.
You cannot miss him
as he struts on the platform
in his red leather boots,
inflating his chest
and stroking his whiskers,
gets the key on his moothie
and renders his favourites,
'O Flower of Cessnock'
and 'Hillhead the Brave'.
Girls come to pat him,
boys shake his paw,
and once he was kidnapped
by an impresario
from Bakerloo
but he sprang his basket
and soon he was back
to yodel at West Street
and dance at Cowcaddens.

THE SUBWAY PIRANHAS

Did anyone tell you
that in each subway train
there is one special seat
with a small hole in it
and underneath the seat
is a tank of piranha-fish
which have not been fed
for quite some time.
The fish become agitated
by the shoogling of the train
and jump up through the seat.
The resulting skeletons
of unlucky passengers
turn an honest penny
for the transport executive,
hanging far and wide
in medical schools.

It's lovely going your holidays on the Glasgow Underground

PARTICK LAUGHS BETTER

Fraser Elder

THE LURE OF the West seems to be universal. In fact, the directional pull is such it would appear almost everyone in the Northern Hemisphere regards West to be best!

Cities of the West are the places where the grass is greener and in turn, the West End of cities throughout the Western world is always synonymous with prestige. Marco Polo was perhaps out of step heading East, presumably to make a mint in China while Christopher Columbus considered the real world to be in the opposite direction. Since then, Pilgrims have, in the main, sought the New World . . . in the West.

And what better a New World . . . than Partick!

To a young man of the East, from the land of Jute and Jam, the Broons and Oor Wullie, Partick appeared to be only a name on a football coupon because of a certain organisation called Thistle. Not so. This young emigré from Dundee was soon to discover that the aforesaid soccer legend was not housed in the district of its title and was nothing more than a masquerade being perpetrated in an outer

. . . lonely as a cloud

limit . . . Maryhill by name. But compensation for a myth being exploded came swiftly as this Dundonian abroad soon discovered that the burgh of Partick—or Pertyck as we naturalised citizens are wont to refer to the district—is actually the Capital of Glasgow.

Thanks to former civic head Dr Michael Kelly, the world was informed Glasgow is Miles Better. That may well be. However, this humble scribe ventures the opinion that Partick is Laughs Better as it is the wonderful, wonderful land of the one-liner.

Soon after folding my tent on the banks of the silvery Tay and journeying to settle adjacent to the cloudy Kelvin with its picturesque marine traffic of mattresses, tyres and Presto trolleys, I became initiated.

"Haw Jim . . . is your name Fraser?"

The query came from a Dalcross Street close-mouth and a denizen emerged when I confirmed the name.

"Aye . . . well I only pit the telly oan when you're aff!"

Hence I was introduced to an art form . . . the Partick put-down.

Back East in Dundee such a counterstroke would be devastating. But in seeking fame and fortune in the West, penalties had to be paid and an education was under way. The time to discard the "Jings, crivvins help ma Boab" image had come. This was now the West End of Glasgow and the real trick was to become a fully-paid-up member as quickly as possible.

To compare life in Partick with Dundee is an awesome task. Once dominated by the three Js—Jam, Jute and Journalism—the Tayside city has undergone major changes and a great deal of the character has drained away. To a degree Glasgow's character has also suffered in the post-war years but has bravely been replaced with an air of enterprise, bringing with it an atmosphere of sophistication and modern-day purpose.

In the midst of it all, the burgh of Partick has doggedly held on to independence and its individuality is there for all to see. Hard times there may be, but in Partick there is a clear pride in coping and laughing at adversity.

Characteristically, Dundee is less capable of adopting a cavalier attitude to the traumas and cynically there is a viewpoint that the effects of the Tay Bridge Disaster of 1879 are still reflected. The town's adopted poet, "Sir" William Topaz McGonagall, with his tortured rhyming and scansion problems, thrived on disaster and was significantly critical of the attitudes of the Dundonians. In reply the city has consistently refused to honour the fact that their very own Bard is a world legend, albeit because of eccentricity.

Politically, the city has always walked hand in hand with controversy and the events of over sixty years ago are known to have been demoralising. Winston Spencer Churchill changed political allegiance during his fourteen years as a city MP and suffered the greatest humiliation of his entire career in 1922 at the hands of a disgruntled population. Folklore hints that the man who later became Prime Minister vowed vengeance on the Tayside city. The explosive politics have continued right to the eighties, culminating with the governing local authority forming links with a West Bank Palestinian city.

While theories abound over the low-key outlook of Scotland's fourth largest city, some answers might be found in how Dundonians view life in the other three. Near neighbours Aberdeen are Scotland's success story, yet only sixty miles away Dundee's lifestyle has generally remained unchanged despite having the North Sea on its doorstep. Edinburgh's phenomenal tourist trade has not greatly affected Dundee, again only sixty miles away, and the men from the East view with some envy the growth of Scotland's foremost commercial centre in Glasgow. In essence the grass appears to be greener everywhere.

Good value at Paddy's

And where greener than good old Partick? The tourist trade is really nothing to speak of . . . oil rigs are fairly thin on the ground . . . five-star hotels are at a premium in Dumbarton Road . . . But here in this part of the West they have one very special commodity in abundance which to a time-served Dundonian is an elixir . . . optimism!

Nowhere but Partick could the following take place.

An early morning postman arrives at Partick Cross traffic lights and at the empty junction he is hailed by an elderly tramp resting on an island in the middle of the road. "Mornin' postie . . . can Ah hiv a word?" The postman carefully crosses the road weighed down by the mail. "Whit is it?" "Anything fir me this moarnin'?"

I am also led to believe by my good friend Billy Connolly Jnr. that Partick can match my home city in terms of a Bard. Discovered by Mr Connolly . . . Elphinstone Filbert McCorkindale . . . as yet unrecognised, apparently penned the work:

> *The snotters dreep fae yon chiel's neb*
> *The glabber skips abin yir thrums*
> *The sleekit stoorie creel's asneck*
> *A' the best son when it comes!*

Music of the pen! Sir William McGonagall, eat your heart out! Partick certainly Laughs Better.

A LIFE OF GLASGOW CRIME

James Donnelly

I DIDN'T KNOW I was a crime reporter till the night I saw my wife sitting at the fireside cleaning a Smith & Wesson .38 revolver which I had picked up in a pub for a fiver, to demonstrate how easy it was to buy guns in Glasgow, after the arrest and execution of Peter Manuel, who had found it quite easy to get a Beretta and a Webley revolver to shoot a couple of families with.

The police, of course, said they had quite a tight rein on the firearms situation in Glasgow, the newspapers said they hadn't, and I was going to prove the latter. I was tipped off to go to a pub in Gorbals, where I was to meet a guy called The Duke. I had been in there for about half an hour when this little chap in a light raincoat came bustling in. He stood at the other end of the bar for a few minutes, and he recognised me because I looked a bit different from the other customers in this establishment. He caught my eye and nodded towards the Gents, and I joined him.

Inside the Gents, he produced the Smith & Wesson, pointed the thing straight at me and fired five times. I was quite glad it was empty. "It's in good working order," he said. "That'll be a fiver." Was there any ammunition, I asked, and he said he could get me ammunition. I asked if he could get any other kind of arms, and he said yes, he could get me a Thomson sub-machinegun, he could get me a Sterling, and so on.

It was only later that I discovered Army barracks were actually raided from time to time, and that's how guns found their way into the underworld. Some years later, in fact, because of that incident, I had occasion to spend two weeks in Ireland, to find out how many guns were finding their way into the hands of the IRA from this country. But it was absolutely minimal. I believe most of the stuff was coming from the States and some parts of the Balkans.

Made for each other

In any case, after meeting The Duke I got acquainted with a guy whom I shall just call Joe, who I think had been quite a good amateur boxer at one time. His parents were divorced, and he seemed to be high-class working-class, if that description means anything. He was nearly an educated man, but he had been in prison a few times, and he was a really hard character. As well as being a safe-blower and a thief, he played the strong-arm man for the big club gangsters in Glasgow, the gambling tycoons. I got to like Joe; in fact, he was such a clean-cut figure, and very amusing to talk to, it was hard to believe he was a jailbird, and had no intention of being anything else. Unlike one or two other old criminals I knew, who were absolutely desperate to become respectable, settle down and get a regular job—not a hard job, but a well-paid job that would enable them to mingle with decent society. They loved coming up to newspaper offices and talking to normal people, or as many normal people as you find in newspaper offices.

(Incidentally, when I talked earlier about the public outcry about guns, it was a newspaper outcry—the public knew nothing about it, till we told them.)

It was Joe who phoned me and asked me if I would like to meet two interesting characters, who turned out to be the most desperate people I ever met in my life. William (Tank) McGuinness and John (Gypsy) Winning. They had blown a safe in a bank in Ayr about a month earlier, and the cops picked them up in a wee house in Cowcaddens with the money stashed under the bed. They hadn't had time to launder it. They were waiting for trial in Barlinnie when they broke out. It was a huge story at the time, and this phone call was to ask me if I wanted to interview them.

I could hardly believe this—even though I used sometimes to get tipped off before bank robberies. I could hardly believe these two could be safely interviewed. The thought that crossed my mind was that I should really tell the police about it, but Joe always reminded me that I had a wife and children, and there was no sense in prejudicing their chances of living, because these people didn't go in for qualms or compunction.

So, I was told to report to a pub in Pollokshaws Road, and I went down there with The Duke. We went into the back room—it was curtained off like a Turkish harem. Sitting there were Joe and the two characters I was meeting for the first time. McGuinness was just a wee overweight Glasgow ned, but Winning was a very striking individual, black hair with a widow's peak and piercing dark eyes that went right through to the back of your skull. He didn't accept a drink, and he didn't smoke, and I wondered, what the hell does he do for relaxation? Does he eat people? He pulled his coat sleeve up to show me his arm, which he had burned getting over the wall. It must have been in agony, beginning to fester, but he was only interested in getting on with this interview, and the reason why he wanted it was in the hope of making fools of the prison officers. He didn't want money, only this odd satisfaction.

While we were sitting there, he noticed something through a crack in the curtains, and he muttered to me to go and have a look at the barman. I had no idea what was going on, but I went outside, and the barman was on the telephone. I stood behind him while he muttered into the phone, he turned round and saw me and went white; then said into the phone—at half-past one in the day—"Do you know the result of the two-thirty?" He was obviously speaking to the police or to somebody who would speak to the police.

So I ordered a taxi, and while we were waiting I phoned my wife in Cathcart and asked her to take the kids for a walk in the park—it was a beautiful sunny day. When the taxi arrived I told Joe we would go out to my house, as a safe place, and not all that far away, and I didn't think any of my respectable neighbours would recognise the chaps.

So Tank and Gypsy lay on the floor of the taxi, and what struck me as funny was the driver didn't seem to see that as anything unusual. He must have recognised these guys; their pictures were all over the papers. They had been in the papers before in connection with other crimes. Gypsy had broken out of Peterhead and lived off the land for a week in the dead of winter. A real hard man, with plenty of headlines to his credit.

When we got to Cathcart another funny thing happened. An elderly neighbour was leaning out of her window enjoying the sunshine, and she said, "Hello there, Jimmy," and I said, "Hello there, Mrs Finlay—lovely day, isn't it?" And Tank and Gypsy said, "Hello, Mrs Finlay, lovely day, isn't it?" "Yes, it's beautiful," and she smiled sweetly at two of the most desperate characters in Britain.

So we went in and I started making tea, and put out the cream cookies. My wife had left out some goodies—she doesn't only clean guns, she can lay a table as well. And Winning said, "Right, when does this story appear?"

I knew it couldn't appear, unless I did something clever like phoning the police and telling them I had agreed to give the criminals five minutes to leave the house. If the story had been printed I would have been on a charge of harbouring criminals, and maybe other things. Winning got quite mad and asked what he was doing in the damned house wasting his time, and I said, "Tell me the story anyway and we'll see." And he was desperate to tell it.

Their story was, they broke out of their cell, crossed the yard, and walked round the wall. Nobody challenged them at all. They were surprised, but they couldn't see an easy way out, so they went back to their cell, where Winning said eff this, we'll have another look. All this, by the way, is designed to make the prison officers look stupid. They went out again, and this time they saw in a corner a heap of timber for some repair work in the prison. They calculated that if they took a run at this and a jump they could reach the top of the wall.

Winning would be the one who could do it, he was the hard man. He did it, McGuinness got a hold of his legs and they climbed over each other. That's when Winning slipped, and slid right down the wall, a fair drop, with his arm rubbing on the stone. It didn't worry him.

I told them I would try to get the story in the *Evening Citizen* on the next day but it would depend on what the editor said, and he might have to do some kind of deal with the police, because I shouldn't have been doing an interview at all. They were impatient, and I called a taxi for the two master-criminals.

Then Joe said he and The Duke would park their taxi at the foot of Albion Street and wait there for their money. Joe was due ten pounds for the introduction,

which wasn't bad, around 1960. I went back to the office, and this is what real life is
in the devil-may-care trade of journalism. I saw the editor and told him I had just
had a fantastic interview, and he said (he was a very nice guy, by the way, Jack
Campbell), "Come in, Jimmy, have a chair." I said I didn't have time, people were
waiting in a taxi and I had to get right out to them, with ten pounds.

"Who are they? What's it all about?"

"Gypsy Winning and Tank McGuinness."

"My God, the people who broke out of Barlinnie?" He pulled two fivers from
his wallet. "Pay them off and don't ever mention this to anybody."

I did, and I'm not sure I should be mentioning it to anybody even yet. I told Joe
the story might be in the paper next day, but that it wasn't up to me.

I met Joe quite a lot, and he used to write to me from Barlinnie, and like nearly
everybody in the criminal fraternity he never bothered to post a letter through the
normal channels. It was a matter of pride to them to have letters smuggled out. In
the same way I received communications from a wee man called Paddy
Meehan—not to be confused with the celebrated Paddy Meehan, just the same
name. This was the last man to be flogged in Britain, flogged twice in fact, and he
wrote to me on a long strip of toilet paper telling me his story and saying he was
coming out soon and would come and see me. I was glad to get rid of him. Sheer
menace. Although he was old, he had the coldest blues I've ever seen. People were
frightened to look at him. I don't know how he had been treated all his life, and
probably that had something to do with it, but I gave him some money and he
went. He was evil.

A year after the Manuel trial I met some interesting people when the papers
were trying to revamp the drama of the investigation into the murders. Two of
them were Joe and Davie. Joe gave evidence against Manuel, and Davie testified on
Manuel's behalf. They were both safe-blowers, and after the trial they committed a
robbery. Joe was allowed to go, and Davie got a year's imprisonment. That's how
the cookie crumbles. . . .

Joe did a long-term undercover job for the police during the investigations,
spending time in Manuel's company, drinking with him and reporting his
movements. He had a code system, because he couldn't be seen near a police
station. When he telephoned he said he was the Quare Fella, and if the police
wanted him to call a beat officer stuck a drawing pin in his door. Joe was able to tell
his detective contact that Manuel was buying drinks with new banknotes. When
these were recovered from the pub, the numbers checked with the pay-packet
stolen from the house in Sheepburn Road where he had murdered the man and
wife and little boy. So Joe had to go into the witness box. A hard thing to do when
your acquaintances are hearing everything. But Joe (a different Joe, by the way,
from the strong-arm character) was a really jaunty guy, and was certainly never
worried about what people thought. He could look after himself.

Then there was John Lafferty, who was important in the Manuel case because
he was with the killer when he was trying out his Beretta by shooting a cow in a
field out in Lanarkshire. And it was found that the slug matched the gun used in the
Sheepburn Road killings. John was not in the same entertaining class as Joe and

. . . nor iron bars a cage

Davie. He lived down in Yorkhill, and this experience gives an insight into the lifestyle of some of my criminal acquaintances. I went down one afternoon to interview him, and he was getting ready to go to the Locarno ballroom. The house was pretty smelly, and it was the first time I actually saw coal in the bath. I had always thought that was a middle-class joke. His wife was ironing his shirt for the dancing, and I didn't particularly want her to be with us all the time during the interview, but when I asked if she was coming along, she said no, she never went to the dancing, he went himself. This man had seven children and there was the wife getting him dolled up for a good time.

We got to the Locarno, and I wanted to get the cow-in-the-field interview over. It turned out he was meeting a woman, nicely dressed, pleasant, respectable lady in her thirties. He was very proud to introduce a genuine reporter to his friend. At some point in the conversation, I unthinkingly said, "That's exactly what your wife was saying an hour ago." The conversation dropped dead. John's face went livid and the lady glared at him. I excused myself, and when I got back she was gone. He explained that he had been courting her for seven years, with the story of a wife in England and a pending divorce.

He had a glass eye, and when he was annoyed he rubbed it, so that it sometimes turned round and made him look like a Greek statue. It frightened me in fact.

There are a few wee sidelights that may give an idea of the psychology of the families of gangsters. I was sent out one Saturday night for the *Sunday Express* to pick up a photograph of a man who had come into the news because he had broken out of jail, or murdered somebody in jail—routine behaviour, really. But the guy was in prison anyway, and it was a house in Maryhill.

I knocked on the door, the woman opened the door, and the living room was absolutely empty. I mean empty. There was no furniture at all. I can't remember what they were sitting on, but there was a child in the corner emptying its bowels, doing the bathroom. Above the mantelpiece there was a big gilt-framed newspaper cutting.

"Oh, are you from the *Express*?"

"That's right. You know he's got into a wee bit trouble?"

"Oh aye, he's always gettin' intae trouble." She sounded quite pleased, she was delighted to see me. "Oh aye, we've got a picture of him here, that's the only one we've got."

It was the gilt-framed cutting, a cutting from a newspaper, of her man being sent to prison for seven years, for some hideous assault. She had gone out and got this thing properly framed, to adorn the fireplace. And it was the only furniture in the room. Nothing else. Maybe a cocktail cabinet in the bed recess, because they always had one of those. But there was no shame, this was a matter of pride that her husband had been in the papers. I didn't know whether to laugh or greet. And I have no theories either. I only tell what happened. Truth is sacred, comment is free, and all that kind C. P. Scott stuff. No comment.

I got pally with a very nice wee safe-breaker— my wife called him Willie fae the Country, and we had him to dinner one night. Really, very good company, Willie, and the only man I ever knew who had been convicted on a toe-print. He had his foot braced against a safe while he worked at it, there was a hole in his sock, and he was done. After dinner he entertained us with long recitations from Kipling, and very well done. Then he said, a bit superciliously to me, "You couldnae dae that." Quick as a flash my wife said, "But Jimmy hasn't had as much time as you to memorise things."

THIS SPORTING LIFE

Ian Archer

THE LATE John Allan, a sportswriter of a previous generation, was once sent down to Liverpool to cover a wartime football international between England and Scotland at Goodison Park. There, Scotland gained a kind of moral victory, even if the dusty old scoreline states factually that England won the match. It's all a question of style. While that particular game hardly represents more than a footnote—wartime internationals not really counting in football statistics—his visit coincided with an important day in the twentieth century. The Luftwaffe bombed the city.

Some three days later, his employers back at the *Daily Record* were becoming understandably worried when he had failed to arrive back in Glasgow. Search parties were sent out. Doubtless an anxious wife was informed. When, somewhat blearily, he turned up at his desk, there was genuine concern. "That must have been awful, John." He sucked on the question for a while with that *gravitas* that always attaches to survivors, before commenting: "It wasn't good. It was probably as bad a defensive performance as I've seen from a Scottish side."

The story must be apocryphal, although you never know. I do know for a fact that six Glaswegians intent on watching a Scotland World Cup match against Israel found the plane fully booked at Heathrow. Denied entry into Tel Aviv, they merely booked for Cairo, knowing it was in the vicinity, and hitchhiked across the desert. At least they had passports. And an acquaintance, en route to the Argentine World Cup, turned up in Lima, Peru (get out the map and work that one out), only to find the capital was at a standstill during a one-day strike. He got out of the airport in what turned out to be a "scab" taxi, which forces of that country's leftish falange tried to set on fire. He was saved from immolation by shouting out of the window, "Fitba, Joe Jordan, Kenny Dalglish." The taxi was waved through, the locals recognising aristocracy even in the middle of the class struggle.

Mute inglorious McMenemys

The patter merchant Johnnie Beattie tells one of my favourite Glasgow stories. In the middle of the slow business of making a film, he wandered into a city pub, deserted apart from a couple of ancients sitting in the corner nursing pints of heavy. The conversation passed quickly through all those stages known to drinking men. It escalated from the discursive, even conspiratorial, to the heated and finally aggressive. One man was doing all the talking. "John," he said, "we've known each other a long time. Our families have married each other. I always thought you were a straight bloke. I never reckoned you'd tell downright lies. But unless you take that back, I'll have to ask you outside. I'm calling you a liar. No one's ever scored a hat-trick in 68 seconds."

Sport is largely played in pubs if it is Glasgow. In the Arlington Bar on Woodlands Road, there is a taxi driver by the name of John Smith who has become modestly famous because of his ability to set sporting posers which baffle even the more respected members of the football *cognescenti*. "Name me an Englishman, an Irishman, a Scotsman and a Welshman all of whom have played for their countries and whose names end in the letter 'I'." Over in the Dry Dock at Scotstoun, you will often find George Mulholland, who actually lives in Toronto, but who doesn't miss many Rangers games. They are just two of a cast of thousands of highly expert football watchers who train on licensed premises.

But rambling anecdote will not do to explain Glasgow and sport. For example, we were up at Firhill one afternoon on the terraces, standing behind a man whose sole contribution was to castigate the then Partick Thistle forward Doug Somner. "Somner," he said, "you're a balloon." Expletives deleted. While encouraging the democratic right to free speech, I felt constrained to tell him that Somner had turned his ankle in training on Thursday and was not in fact playing. "Sorry son," he replied, "I lost my glasses on Thursday and, to be honest, I can't even see the pitch." I asked him why he bothered. Crushingly, he gave me a withering look and added: "Because I haven't missed a game in seventeen years."

But the point of that story is that it is not the point. Glasgow has lost its appetite for football. It is a city which can increasingly live without it. To proclaim it any longer as the capital of the football world is absurd. It may cherish honourable traditions and it has certainly made its mark on the sport in a way which only half a dozen cities—Rio, Turin, Milan, Liverpool, Manchester and Madrid—can hope to emulate. But its glories are fading. They may rise again, but never with the same passions, the same weight of numbers. Glasgow has grown up and can see beyond the touchlines.

As I write, a Glaswegian, Robert Millar, has just finished riding in the 1984 Tour de France, that snakes and ladders of a cycling race in which a whole country is the board on which it is run. He finished fourth, the highest ever place by a Brit, and was King of the Mountains. Even the posh papers say that he comes from the Gorbals, a word which casts doubt over the veracity of those reports. Anyway, the point is that as a boy, Millar was walking down Argyle Street when he stopped at a shop window and watched the TV which was showing the same Tour de France. "When I grow up, I'm going to ride in that," he said to himself. And he did so. Now the old myth about Glasgow is that he would have been branded as an effete just for contemplating a

Walter McGowan

sport which wasn't football or boxing, or both and preferably at the same time.

True, I do not ever expect any Olympic equestrian team to contain a member who was born in Easterhouse but the point is that we have broadened our horizons. We no longer keep our eye on the ball as it lies on the deck. We look up, around us, and outward.

There were always those who did so. Tom Weir put on thick socks and walked out of Springburn towards the hills. But increasingly, the point has been taken by Glaswegians that any accident of birth is not a disqualification from taking part in any sport and doing it well. I find this attitude far more enlightening than anything which the city's football clubs may or may not achieve, inside or outside of Europe, or even Aberdeen.

That there was a wee bit more to life than an accurate cross to the far post was recently proved by no less an august personage than Bailie Jean McFadden. Believing, like most Glaswegians, that what happens in the Council Chambers is at best an embarrassment and even an impertinence to the way that the rest of us live in this city, I am not entirely sure what exact obligations Ms McFadden has to the small caucus of voters who gave her permission to run our affairs. But she seems a decent enough wee soul. A few months ago, West of Scotland Cricket Club at Hamilton Crescent looked like going bust. It is not only a famous cricket club but its ground was the sight of the first-ever football international played in the world. The committee looked for support, and found it in Ms McFadden, that denizen of the left who promised ratepayers cash.

At first sight this was strange. Labour politicians do not court the cricket vote in the same way that American Democrats weigh in the Italians or the Jews. Dutifully, she made inquiries into the fact that the club was not a hotbed of elderly members getting stoshous on large pink gins in front of framed portraits of Winston, Monty, HRH and Mrs Thatcher. No, she discovered, they provided important community facilities. They were to be saved.

It was a nice piece of politics, but she gave it all away by adding: "When I was a wee girl, I liked to go down there and watch the cricket." In that she did more for her city, and the solid ranks of Labour placemen who guide our destinies, than anything for years. It broke the image. It destroyed the myth that everyone round here who was under five-foot-two could become the next Benny Lynch and that if you had not been seen falling about fu' on the terraces of Hampden Park, Ibrox or Parkhead, then you were not a man, my son. We had a lady who liked her cricket and who would do a wee bit for it.

Actually, Glasgow has been doing quite a lot for sport since they set up an unpaid quango called the Glasgow Sports Promotions Council a decade ago. The idea was to attract top-class sports to the city and to provide adequate facilities for them to be played. Thus Jim Watt was allowed to become World Lightweight Champion in front of his own people, and Bernhard Langer and Ken Brown were to become the first two winners of the Glasgow Golf Championship. The list is extensively longer than that and will grow when the Silver Broom curling world championship comes to the city. When that spider's web of steel on the old Queen's Dock becomes an exhibition centre, then maybe we will get the top tennis players and gymnasts and all varieties of sportsmen competing there. So where's your football now?

Then there is the Glasgow Marathon, which is not only the third largest exercise in human jogging in the world and which, annually, closes the Sabbath City down as 10,000 run up Maryhill Road and over the Temple, down the Switchback and on to the Clydeside Expressway, before turning on to the south side and its strange places. Not only that, the year-long struggle to fitness fills the pavements up during spring and summer. The Glaswegian in his Nike shoes plodding the lonely miles has not just become a traffic hazard but also a sweating symbol of life away from the boozer, the betting shop and the terraces.

Still, much needs to be done. At places like Bearsden and Bishopbriggs, they built sports centres, temples to a new world where Maw, Paw and the weans could swim and play badminton. These have encouraged participation in sports largely unknown before TV brought them into the living room. There is no need to join exclusive private clubs to indulge. Some distant historian may well see them as good and honourable places in an age which was anything but good and honourable; but how much better it would have been if they had been built in those parts of the old Glasgow where urban renewal was proclaiming a bright future for a new city.

So farewell, Glasgow football—or not quite. It was, after all, four Glaswegians who confronted us in Copenhagen, two hours after a Scotland game there. They decanted from a taxi with the immortal line, "Hey Jimmy, when does the match start?" There will still be a feeling for the game in the old town, poorly though those fans have been treated down the years.

The SFA make loud noises about Hampden Park, still the place where all the European crowd records were set up, but in reality they are patching together a monument rather than creating a vision of the future. Rangers insist that anyone can play for them but refuse to translate that promise into fact. They built a fine stadium but are still looking for a team to play in it. Celtic, in their great years, didn't make Parkhead anything more than a down-market place of entertainment. Partick Thistle have flirted with playing in some distant place called East Kilbride. The dogs matter more at Shawfield. Queen's Park lives, an anachronism.

As a boy, I marvelled as to how Maryhill Road would fill on a Saturday afternoon. Half the excitement in going for a lift over the turnstiles lay in the knowledge that one shared the experience with a large bulk of that neighbourhood's mankind. The terraces were tough, cheerful places, packed tight. Now only small cadres of those with nothing better to do make the same pilgrimages. We take our young ones, hoping that a little of it will rub off. Mostly now, wee boys prefer to play—and a generation, as well as a constituency, has been lost.

The reasons are well explained over the years. When the ordinary man was no longer required to work Saturday morning and stay out of the house while the wife cleaned in the afternoon, the writing was on the wall. Then, houses with central heating and racing on the box hastened the decline. There was more to do and football became just a bit—an important bit—of folklore, not its central canon. We grew up and grew older and suddenly the heroes were that bit smaller.

I still know that the four players whose names ended in an "I" were Macari, Bonetti, Kryswicki and Mancini; and in the pubs the talk will take its usual turn towards events of the football day. There are some great players around still and some matches are intrinsically thrilling. There's not much wrong with football but the new Glasgow has put it in its context. It is no longer, in contradiction to the words of the late Bill Shankly, a somewhat more important matter than life and death. It's a game and a good one, not to be neglected but no longer to be revered.

"KEEP THE HEID!"

Rikki Fulton

VIEWING AS I do each year the approach of the annual "Old Firm" game with mounting apprehension, I fell recently to pondering some of the more interesting scores of the recent and historic past. For example...1948: Rangers 39—Celtic 15;

Some species of sporting event or other

1957: Rangers 17—Celtic 51. Not *GOALS*, you understand—*BODIES ON THE TERRACING!*

So much thought has been given to the problem of soccer violence—so much time and effort spent, and yet we seem no closer to a solution. And it's not always confined to the hallowed ground itself. Take the tartan-bedecked giant in the pub before the game, for instance. "Hey, *JIMMY*," he rifts down his pint tumbler. "You a Rangers supporter?" Now the chances of answering this one correctly and coming out of the pub with your face intact are not great. If you say "yes", your teeth could be made redundant because he *DOESN'T* support Rangers. And if you say "no", your nose could be introduced to your chin because he *DOES!* And if you try something crafty like, "I support Thistle, actually," you could be on your way to the morgue because he thinks you're making fun of him. *AND HE'S NOT EVEN GOING TO THE MATCH!*

So what is it about this game that arouses such deep emotion, such aggression, such violence? Is there an answer?

Certainly great strides have been made by those lumbered with the preservation of law and order in learning to detect those little tell-tale signs of possible unrest. For example: *"HEY, JIMMY! 'AT WIS MA PIE YE JIST STOOD OAN"* . . . or . . . *"HEY, JIMMY! AH HOPE FUR YOUR SAKE AT'S HOT BOVRIL AT'S RUNNIN' DOON MA LEG!"* . . . or . . . *"HEY, JIMMY, GIE'S SOME ------' ROOM FUR ----'S SAKE!"*

But this, as they say, is small beer. We're not concerned with the occasional, almost polite, little confrontation on the terracing. We're talking about great hordes of screaming, fighting men, blood and guts akimbo, eyes staring, mouth and flies agape, rampaging down through the terracing and on to the pitch itself. (Whence comes, of course, the term "pitched battle".)

Well, IS there an answer? Can we even begin to understand it? *OF COURSE WE CAN'T.* The simple truth is that violence has been there all the time. *IT'S THE FOOTBALL THAT'S NEW!*

Bringing home the pot

According to *Britannica* the game of football has its origins in Ancient Britain, and owes its development to "man's instinctive desire to kick any small object in his path". (This can be anything from an empty beer can to a wee wumman out for the messages.) Legend has it that the first-ever football used was the head of a dead Danish brigand. (Or if he wasn't dead at kick-off, he almost certainly was after the first penalty.) But the game, you see, was simply a way of celebrating a victory over one's enemies. (Incidentally, there is little evidence to support the theory that the game was known originally as *"KEEP THE HEID!"*) But the point is that as it grew in popularity it became something of a headache. And not just for the gent who provided the ball.

In earlier centuries many a battle was held up as the opposing infantrymen indulged in their passion for the game rather than kill each other for King and Country. Indeed, one thirteenth-century Scottish writer, having witnessed one of these unexpected Cup Finals, was moved to report that the Anglo-Scottish war (which began in 1297) was *"NOT BEING TAKEN WITH A PROPER SERIOUSNESS BY EITHER PARTY"*. In 1365 Edward III, with similar problems, decided to *"PROHIBIT FOOTBALL FOR MILITARY REASONS"*. These facts give us a much clearer understanding of the problem of soccer violence and bring us back to the maxim I offered earlier. *VIOLENCE HAS BEEN THERE ALL THE TIME. IT'S THE "GAME" THAT IS NEW!* In all humility, therefore, I offer the following as a possible solution.

At all future matches simply plant both teams, referee, linesmen, managers and directors in the *STAND* and let them watch the fans fight it out on the field.

We've got it the wrong way round, you see. We shouldn't be trying to eliminate the *VIOLENCE . . . ELIMINATE THE FOOTBALL*, that's what's causing all the trouble.

Phoenix-like

MY KIND OF TOWN

Tony Queen

ONE THING I know about Glasgow is that it's a place where a man can get on, especially if enough people are soft enough to think they can beat the bookie. I have to smile when I hear about some punter making a big killing. He doesn't mention the times he lost his shirt. But on top of that, the fascination in the gambling game is that it takes in every level of society, it's a world in miniature with everybody from dossers to company directors living out their dreams.

I never thought of any other trade, although my old man never made much of it when he was taking lines for a bookie, and the *dolce vita* in those days was seven of us in a single-end. My mother was from Ireland, and she lived and died without learning to read or write, but I learned a lot from her. One thing was to speak the truth and shame the devil, and it does pay. Telling lies is like fiddling your golf score. Who are you conning? Yourself.

The other thing was her passion for education, although she had none, or maybe because she had none. I started school at St Joe's and got a scholarship to St Aloysius, and I stuck at it. I was pretty good, especially in English and arithmetic, and they're the things that matter most—except maybe music. I wanted to study

Is it a bird? Is it a plane?

music, but on that level of society you were lucky to get a moothie, never mind a piano.

The funny thing is that I might have been a career soldier. When I was called up during the war, I was sent to the Pay Corps in Edinburgh, which I thought was a bit shaming till the news of casualties started coming in, and suddenly Edinburgh looked pretty good. Hardly any soldiers got shot in Edinburgh. The C.O. was very keen that I should stay on after the war, get a commission and go far, but I just wanted to be a bookie.

It was illegal, of course. You have to laugh when you think that betting shops in Glasgow were strictly against the law—but you got planning permission to set one up. We were raided regularly as a matter of form, bundled along to court with the customers, and the routine was that we paid their fines and slipped them a half-note.

If we got wind of a raid, and we did, we sometimes let the punters vanish if they chose, and dragged in old age pensioners to go through the routine and pick up ten bob. Everybody was happy, but it was a crazy situation. We have to have law and order, but nobody can pass a law that makes people good, cures their personal vices. And Glasgow today is a lot more sensible.

I live out in Milngavie, of course.

COMING TO GLASGOW

Georg Heuser

I HAD WANTED to come to Glasgow for many years. Or rather I had wanted to come to Scotland, but as the Goethe Institute's branch office for Scotland happens to be in Glasgow, this meant going there. I had joined the Goethe Institute at the beginning of 1970 and had put my wishes on record at the first opportunity. But when after two years a transfer seemed imminent, to my disappointment, someone who had endured the hardships of life in the tropics was sent there to enjoy the comfort of a milder climate. Sad to say, this moderate climate did not agree with him and he left after only two years—with rheumatism.

My interest in Scotland sprang from many sources. As a child I had read novels by Sir Walter Scott in German translation and thus become acquainted with some aspects of Scottish history. Like most other Germans I knew, through a popular ballad by Theodor Fontane, of the Tay Bridge Disaster and the death of so many unfortunate travellers. Shakespeare's *Macbeth* had given me another glimpse of Scottish history. Duncan, Glamis, Cawdor and Macduff had become familiar names, although for many years I pronounced them in a peculiar, i.e. a very German, way. Like everybody else I had heard of clans and tartans, whisky and Bonnie Prince Charlie.

Scottish Opera, the City's Finest

In the early fifties, as a student in England, I had twice included Scotland in my grand tour of Britain, first hitchhiking and then cycling. Thus I got to see Melrose Abbey and Abbotsford, Edinburgh Castle and Holyrood House Palace, the Forth Bridges, the City of Granite and Inverness, Loch Ness and Loch Lomond, Fort William and Glencoe. I had miserably failed to conquer Ben Nevis on a rainy day when the soles of my boots came off, and I had only had a glimpse of Glasgow through which I travelled after dusk. I had been pleased with the discovery that there lived people in the British Isles who did not only write but also pronounced r's, people who even could pronounce "loch" and "ach" properly.

When reading literature at my *alma mater*, I had learned about the enormous impact the Ossian fragments, published by Macpherson, had had on continental literature in the second half of the eighteenth century, and about Goethe's involvement with pirate editions printed in Germany at the time of Napoleon's blockade.

The Scotsmen I had met abroad had, with one exception, been very pleasant people, and none of them, to my surprise, had shown any signs of meanness (I did not know, then, that this cliché is for the most part an invention of Sir Harry Lauder). This observation was corroborated by a German diplomat in Istanbul who congratulated us on our decision to go to Scotland and told us that he and his wife had been surprised to discover that during their term of duty at the embassy in London ten out of the dozen or so close friends were Scots.

So I had already formed some impressions of Scotland, but what did I know about Glasgow? Well, as a boy I was crazy about ships, and when browsing through

Rogues and vagabonds

those fascinating illustrated books on maritime vessels, which are the delight of boys of all ages, I had found that most of the great liners and big battleships had been built on the Clyde. This had led me to the logical conclusion that Glasgow was the biggest shipbuilding centre in the world and a great industrial city.

I had also come to know that it had been in Glasgow where a man whose name sounded like Vat had conceived the idea of the steam engine when watching a kettle boiling. I had, however, found it difficult to reconcile this information with the fact that a plaque on a memorial fountain in Kassel, my home town, claimed that a certain Denis Paplin had invented the steam engine and also successfully experimented with a steamboat on the river Fulda "near this place". And all this apparently in the century before James Watt was born.

There seemed to be no doubt, on the other hand, about the genuineness of the claim of a scientist called Kelvin, apparently another Glasgow man, to have made important contributions to physics. That a certain Joseph Lister had founded antiseptic surgery when working in Glasgow and Edinburgh hospitals I had learned from a young student of medicine, later to become my wife.

The importance of Glasgow as a shipbuilding centre was also brought home to me when in Istanbul where I discovered plaques saying "Clyde built" on many of the passenger ferries serving the stations along the Bosphorus and the Sea of Marmora. When about to leave Istanbul and discussing the move to Glasgow we learned that there were two famous football teams in Glasgow, Celtic and Rangers, and that they were great rivals. This was common knowledge among our Turkish friends, but had been unknown to us till then. When actually meeting supporters of Celtic and Rangers in Glasgow it struck me that the rivalry between the fans of these two teams might well be compared with the bloody rivalry existing between the factions of the Blues and the Greens in sixth-century Constantinople. (In Istanbul, incidentally, I also learned from a professor of the Fine Arts University that a satellite town by the name of Cumbernauld was regarded as one of the outstanding examples of twentieth-century town planning.)

What I actually experienced when I came to Glasgow with my family in April 1981 can only be described as a succession of pleasant surprises. There was an unexpected wealth of excellent Georgian and Victorian architecture in that supposedly ugly city, and there were more parks than in any great town I knew. The smoke and smog we had expected no longer existed. The collection of treasures in the museums and art galleries were likewise astonishing.

Cathedral calm at Kelvingrove

The rich religious life in this bustling city with four cathedrals and ever so many churches made us feel quite at home, while the quantity and quality of musical and theatrical events left us literally gasping. To find an Opera and a Ballet, a National Orchestra and an Early Music Consort, a music and drama academy and Britain's most exciting and most controversial theatre, The Citizens, all in one place was beyond my wildest dreams.

There were two universities and the largest college of education in Britain, excellent public libraries and a good newspaper with a great tradition, gorgeous civic buildings and a charming toy-like underground. Soon after our arrival we witnessed the coming into being of the Glasgow Theatre Club and preparations for the now firmly established Mayfest.

All this and much more has, of course, been observed and more aptly described by other newcomers and visitors. I should like to add, however, what may seem a rather trivial observation, but is to somebody coming from Turkey a rather important fact, namely that the quality of the drinking water in Glasgow is superior to that of any other city I know and is only matched, if at all, by that of a few famous wells in and outside Istanbul.

And lastly, I want to state that Scots in general and Glaswegians in particular are as friendly and nearly as helpful as the Turks, who in my opinion are the best of neighbours to be found anywhere. My family and I have found that indeed Glasgow's miles better. Or, to modify a quotation from Schiller's *Maria Stuart: Glasgow ist besser als sein Ruf!*

We gave the streets back to the people, and see what they did with them

THE GREAT BUD

Ranald MacColl

IMAGINE, IF YOU will, two matrons in a park. They are standing before daffodils and, like Wordsworth, their thoughts are moved to a loftier plane by the beauty of the blooms. It could be a springtime scene anywhere: "For yellieness ye cannae bate a daffy. As yelly as yelly. There's nothing yellier than a guid daffy if ye like yelly . . ." Correction, it could only be in Glasgow.

"Well, whit are ye sitting doon tae be up tae noo?"

No book on Glasgow could really be complete without mention of one of her own sons, whose perception and creative draughtsmanship so concisely encapsulated the Keelie culture. Bud Neill was born, as he would have it, around the turn of the century, the youngest son of a poor Glasgow woodchopper who lived in a clearing in the forest and made utility wardrobes. His birth certificate tells another story. He first saw the light of day on 4 April 1911, in the parish of Partick, and was dubbed William Neill. But little William was not to dally long in the dear green city for, after three months, his father's work commitments uprooted the Neill family to Troon. Most of his formative years were to be spent recovering from ruptures, ringworm, tonsilitis, appendicitis and almost every other "itis" in the book, with the occasional interruption to attend Troon Higher Grade School.

He was, by his own admission, no scholar. But he was an inveterate doodler and he whiled away his schooling hours daubing his exercise books with renderings of motorbikes and wee men and wimmen, receiving many "highly commendeds" for the covers of his jotters.

So it was a thankful Billie who left school after third grade with barely a curt nod from the headmaster on the way out as an endorsement of his years at Troon

Higher Grade. Two years later, after a lengthy talk with his father regarding his future—"He could see by then that I was burning with ambition to live off him for the rest of my life"—and after dismissing the possibility of following in his hero William S. Hart's footsteps, for there was not much of a living to be made as a cowpuncher in Troon, Bud opted for a four-year stint in a Commercial Art course at the Glasgow School of Art. On leaving there, his first attempts at commercial art proved unsuccessful. Glaswegians were not to recognise Bud's quirky genius for another decade.

In the late thirties the Neills decided to "flit" to Vancouver, B.C., Canada, but after a year returned to Britain. Life proper started when at the tender age of twenty-seven he decided to pack his hanky and run away from home.

He worked as a petrol pump attendant and chauffeur, then, on the outbreak of war, became a "civvy-attached" driver of army medical supplies and, soon afterwards, went north to join the Army. Although passed as fit to serve in His Majesty's Armed Forces as No. 556507 Gnr. Neill, W., R.A., he was discharged a year later suffering from an ulcer: "There were so many of the boys discharged

"Somehow fush aye reminds me o' the sea . . ."

with the same complaint that we finally called the Battery the King's Own Duodenal Ulcers."

As a civvy again he had a stab at undertaking but "it was a dead-end job". He finally came to rest, bus-driving with S.M.T. Reading a letter to the editor in the *Glasgow Herald* one morning, which called for the disciplining of bus drivers who ran past stops, so incensed Bud that he penned a pithy reply in defence of his colleagues. The remarkable letter impressed the *Herald* editor and he asked Driver Neill for an interview during which Bud suggested he could also "draw a bit". "Our City" cartoon series first appeared in the *Evening Times* on January 10, 1944, by Bud Neill (Bud was a childhood sobriquet given to him by his elder brother). It was an immediate success.

"Line's awfy bad. Cannae make oot if he's got a wee cauf,
a week off, or a wee cough . . ."

These cartoon cameos, daily depicting the peculiarities of the Glaswegian culture, were voraciously devoured by the *Evening Times* readers. Those hardy perennials—his wee wimmen—are timeless, their bulk, that would be the envy of a Sumo wrestler, enveloped in wall-to-wall coats and topped off with the inevitable bun hats. They stand on street corners laden with shopping bags, the occasional wean tucked underarm with all the adeptness of a scrum-half, engrossed

"Run doon tae Princes Street an' get ma pie, son.
It rolled oot ma haun . . ."

in conversations whose subjects range from Shakespeare to shoogly legs—"It's aboot a lot o' blokes in nightgoons stabbin' some auld joker wi' a crew cut, and the patter's wicked . . ." (Julius Caesar). The reader would turn to page two of the newspaper and eavesdrop a recurring topic of these impromptu al fresco chinwags—"Hello, Mrs Thompson. An' whit are ye near deid wi' this morning?" or, perhaps, overhear a description of one of their menfolk—"Och, ye ken him. Big bushy moustache wi' knock-knees receding at the temples . . ."

Bud wasted none of his experiences among his Glasgow people. His bus driver years were revisited as in the cartoon of a "clippie" giving a rookie "clippie" the full benefit of her long mileage on the buses—"Well aff ye go. An' mind it's the public ye're dealin' wi' an' no wi' onythin' intelligent . . ."

His natural off-beat humour, penchant for the written word and "rerr lug for the patter" became the ingredients of many classic one-liners and short poems. A

Awfy clever wean, this. Say 'Awa an bile yir heid' that ye learnt aff the budgie, hen . . ."

"Haw, Jennifer! Ma kirby's fell doon a stank . . ."

"Okey-dokey, Toamy, Aff we go intae the wide blue yonder . . ."

Portrait of Mrs Thomson officially opening the Toonheid windae-hingin' season.

wee wumman and wean inquire of a blazered yachtsman on Rothesay Pier:
"Yaffayat? Whityatyaff?"

Bud also gave us the much quoted laconic story of "Wee Josie" who was
standing at a bus stop being subjected to the rigours of a Scottish winter's night. It
was headed "Bud's Perishing Pome, specially haun wrote" and continued:

> *Winter's came, the snow has fell,*
> *Wee Josie's nose is froze as well,*
> *Wee Josis frozis nosis skintit*
> *Winter's diabolical . . . intit?*

One of his own favourite poems was:

> *The snowdrop drips, the crocus croaks,*
> *And in my little window box*
> *A yelly daffy hings its heid,*
> *It does indeed.*
> *Oh, daffy must you hing your heid?*
> *Could you but heid your hing*
> *Nae bother wid it be tae rhyme*
> *Your heiding hing with Spring.*

But it was undoubtably in his creation of the small town of Calton Creek,
somewhere in the Arizona desert, a ragtag patchwork of humanity, that his
popular, oblique sense of humour reached new heights. "Lobey Dosser" is, at first
sight, a series of western yarns in the classic mould: white hat, sheriff's
badge—goody; black hat and apparel—baddie; but things aren't quite as they seem
for the formula has been given the Neillian twist. The people walking the boards
of "the Creek" talk with a distinct Glasgow accent! "Lobey Dosser", the town
sheriff and hero, has Springburn connections (he ran away to sea at an early age).
He is an honest and forthright little man who barely comes up to John Wayne's
knee when he pulls himself up to his full height, but nevertheless has a big heart.

His name is adapted from lobby dosser—an appellation applied to the
homeless men of the city who used to sleep (doss) on the wooden-floored top
landings (lobbies) of the older tenements. He keeps his "guid eye", keener than a
bucketful of eagles' eyes, on "the Creek", thwarting the various nefarious plots
engineered by the resident crook "Rank Bajin". Lobey's constant companion is also
his means of transportation—the two-legged wonder-horse El Fideldo (Elfie).
Why a two-legged steed? One theory bandied about is that Elfie's great-great-
great-grandfather, a donkey, had the misfortune to be owned by a constant
bletherer and consequently lost his back legs. But Bud himself had a simpler
answer: "It's easier to draw a two-legged horse than a four-legged horse."

Bud's favourite character in these gun-snorting dramas is the totally
unscrupulous villain of the set, Rank Bajin. If Lobey is mongrel, Bajin is pedigree.
He is a silver-tongued rogue of some style who has obviously had the educational
advantages denied the sheriff. These two protagonists are aided and abetted by a

cast of thousands, including Toofy Teeth, chief of the local Injun tribe; Adoda Glorr, daughter of rancher Whisk E. Glorr and breaker of Lobey's heart; Rid Skwerr, a foreign spy and part-time official haunter of the Creek's graveyard; Honey Perz, the local talent and niece of Vinegar Hill, a homesteader; Fairy Nuff, a Yoker lassie with some pantomime experience, and many more too humorous to mention. Lobey became not only a hero in Calton Creek but also in his city of origin where the people took him, his acquaintances and Bud Neill to their hearts.

From the first appearance of Lobey Dosser in the Glasgow *Evening Times,* even respectable businessmen in impeccably upper-class suits jostled with one another to grab the paper from newsvendors, a sight rarely seen since the belated announcement of the relief of Mafeking. And since that date, and since William Neill, there has never been anything like Bud Neill. And there never will be...

SNOBS AND SCRUFF

Cliff Hanley

IT IS OFTEN asserted, even by me, that the class thing never got off the ground in Glasgow, and that we are all Jock Tamson's bairns. A close examination, all the same, reveals that the city is not completely without aspirations to social and cultural superiority to the Joneses, and certainly to the McGlumphers, scruffy gets every one of them.

The world would be a lot less fun without snobbery, the most harmless of vices, and thank God we have our share. In a way, it's one of our entrance tickets to the human race. I shouldn't have been flabbergasted, though I was, when I discovered recently that there were social strata in Greenock—Greenock, for heaven's sake, that grimy wee town whose only function is to lead from Glasgow to Gourock pier!

It was Roy Hanlon, the strolling mountebank, who recalled that when he attended Greenock Academy he was at some pains to lie that he lived in the West End of town. When some cheeky first-form tick did a bit of foul espionage and reported that the Hanlon house was up a close away to the east, Hanlon shifted his ground and said that it wasn't in the East End, but in Central Greenock, and what's more, several university professors, millionaire tycoons and such-like, lived up the same close.

The same Hanlon around that period spent an annual holiday with an aunt in Fife, of whom he stood in great awe because she was the acknowledged leader of the social set in Kirkcaldy. Yes, Kirkcaldy, the Marbella of the East.

We take it for granted that snobbery is the staple industry of Edinburgh, and certainly there are many engaging tales from Auld Reekie, like that of the elegant lady window-shopping at Jenner's, who became disagreeably conscious of a female

Buchanan Street scene

person openly peering at her. She began to fear some disaster, like a dropped hem on her musquash, but in the end the female person leapt forward and said: "It is you! Mrs Miller from Corstorphine!" The lady's huffy retort was purest Edinburgh. "Quite the contrary!"

All right, the sowl. But we can match the story with a real-life experience of a Glasgow lady on a bus bound eastward towards Byres Road, and being aware of a female person behind her, not at all the type one would expect to meet in Highburgh Road, and presumably some kind of cleaner arrangement, a mere visiting menial; presumably also a granny from the grubby child being dandled on her knee. It's only a short bus ride, thought the lady. One can put up with life's annoyances as long as they're brief. But at that moment an acrid smell assailed her, and squinting over her shoulder she discovered that the granny had given the brat a half-peeled orange, which the little ogre was rubbing experimentally on the lady's fur collar. Before she could think of a suitably stunning rebuke, the granny cried, "Stoap that, you'll get your orange a' herry!"

Oh, it all adds to the warp and whatsitsname, the rich thingummy of life. And I have to confess that I grew up infused with snobbery. If you imagine that being one of a family of nine, growing up in a two-room-and-kitchen in the Gallowgate, must preclude any social pretensions, you just don't know the snobbery game. We all need to know that there's somebody worse off than we are, somebody we're entitled to sneer at, even if we try to sneer sympathetically.

The Hanleys were respectable. The Gilligans (name changed to protect the innocent) were scruff.

It wasn't because the five-year-old Gilligan would, on request, eat worms. That was his party trick, and much admired, in a boaky sort of way. The reason why the Gilligans were scruff was . . . I've got to get this right . . . was because the Gilligans were scruff, for God's sake, it's perfectly obvious when people are scruff.

It would be nasty to record that they wore parish suits. It would ill become a prole to scoff at honest poverty. Some high Tories do regard poverty, and unemployment, as a wilful self-inflicted wound. Such blasphemy could never be entertained by another of Jock Tamson's bairns. (Research has established, by the way, that Jock Tamson was a primaeval Pict with a ten-speed bike and a prodigious libido.) But to hell, we entertained such blasphemy.

The small male Gilligans also had heads shaven into the wid, with a cow's lick left at the front. They would grease this and torture it into a wee wave in an attempt to pass for white, but we knew that the bowl haircut was meant to reduce the possible habitat of passengers. And flaes and poolies were definitely the mark of the scruff.

The fact that we kept a bone-comb was irrelevant. Ah, the dear old bone-comb. I was forced regularly to kneel on the floor while my mother dragged this hellish thing down my scalp to dislodge a shower of tiny creatures on to a newspaper, and thence into the fire where they perished with a very satisfying little pistol shot. No matter—in fact, our very possession of a bone-comb raised us above the miserable level of the Gilligans, and cut out the need for the shameful Cherokee coiffure. A head of hair had a social cachet.

They don't make them like that any more

At the same time, we admitted only grudgingly that some people might be superior to us. The King, okay, and he didn't spend a lot of time in the Gallowgate to sneer at us. The minister, all right, as long as he didn't come too strong. The doctor, fair enough. Schoolteachers were a complex case. The relationship was so often one of hate-hate that they were just beasts from another planet, but at the same time, education was the game, certainly in my family, and you had to give a grudging respect to people who had got their heads crammed with it right up to the top, the Three Rs squirting out of their ears.

The matter of education had a serious importance, I now realise. Scruff don't think much of it except as an interruption to peever or leave-oh. That was a sure sign. My mother left school at twelve, but I never heard her make a grammatical mistake, and anybody who did was decidedly down-market, and probably scruff even if they couldn't help it.

Language has always been a marvellous snob thing, of course. We did use a lot of Scots vocabulary, preferred oxters to armpits and stanks to gratings, and Scots forms like doon the dunny—"down" sounded pretentious, and so did "girl" for the correct "lassie". But the cases and tenses were always correct, and we never seen things or done things, we saw them and did them.

Kids have an astonishing ability to cope with linguistic variations on that social level. I grew up trilingual, with a decent Doric for home use, gutter Glasgow for the streets, and the King's English for school, and never got them transposed. The scruff did. One of them in my Penny Buff actually said cludgie to the teacher's face, an astonishing gaffe. Yes, you could pick out a scruff by the chat. They were positively not material for silk purses.

It baffled me later to find that some people lived in houses without books. We were falling over them, and every one devoured, however abstruse or irrelevant. Later on, in my teens, my mother called the attention of a visiting cousin to the new bookcase she had bought for me on the never-never in Smart's. He looked impressed enough, and asked if the books came with it. Palpable scruff. He was a relation on my father's side, of course. That clinched it with my mother, though the old man himself fairly ate books.

In the earlier days, though, it was certainly a dazzling experience to meet an actual Lady, right in our kitchen, and there was no questioning that degree of superiority. We'll call her Lady Hamilton, because I think that was her name—not yon Lady Hamilton, another one—and she had something to do with good works and visitations of mercy for the church. She transformed my view of the world, that's for sure. I had always felt sorry for God because He didn't have a second name like everybody else, and suddenly it clicked. If she was Lady Hamilton, He must be Lord Hamilton. My nimble mind was able to accept this simultaneously with the discovery, not peculiar to me, that He was Harold Wishart, as in Our Father Wishart in Heaven, Harold be Thy name.

I digress, again. Language also had inverted dangers, for people who set out to increase their social stature by a cubit by taking thought. They were the kind who took the ashes down to the midding in neatly tied paper parcels, and talked about the bathroom when you knew they had only a cludgie like everybody else. They

Rich!

were properly dismissed as Lace curtains an' nae sheets on the bed, or Pease brose
an' piannas, or Fur coat an' nae drawers, and their speech was a trip through a
minefield, with lemming sole for tea, pitting the kettle on for to bile, and playing
the car anglais.

The generic Glasgow term is Kelvinside or pan-loaf or wally close, though in a
school debate I once referred to Knightswood English, a simple confusion caused
by the fact that the green car was labelled Knightswood via Kelvinside. They could
both have been Ultima Thule as far as I knew.

Kelvinside, however, is not a place (though it is), but a state of mind, and we
can find this interesting dialect, if we have strong stomachs, in little pockets of
the East End and even the dreaded South Side where, I was brought up to accept,
they eat their young. You may in fact deeply offend some Glaswegians if you
accuse them of being Kelvinsiders when they actually live in the vastly superior
Hillhead; and there are some who suspect that the Hillhead constituency elected
Roy Jenkins, not for his stalwart qualities and political vision, but because he talks
posh.

When my family moved from the tenements to the little Corporation housing
scheme of Sandyhills, we would not have called the King our uncle, and no doubt
he was glad of that. We did feel that the social turmoil was over for people who
had a house with a whole garden, and running hot and cold water for the bath,
though that bit didn't impress me a lot.

Next to godliness

We were wrong, of course. The stratification went on stratifying People in semis were clearly a cut above those in terraces, and more so those in two-up-two-downs. Then another bizarre division arose.

Sandyhills is bisected East to West by the Shettleston Burn, a pleasant stream which I used a lot for falling into; and some of the earnest social pushers at Eastbank Academy (Academy! You want to see the place!) produced the theory that the very name Sandyhills applied only to the half of the scheme to the south of the burn, which is certainly hillier than the other half and has Sandyhills Golf Club. We peasants on the north side could claim only to live in Shettleston. The houses were identical, but obviously there is an inherent superiority in the word Sandyhills, and any linguist will tell you the arrangement of letters in Shettleston is socially debased. The better word must not be cheapened by illegitimate usage by the disenfranchised.

Shettleston itself is a fairly venerable tenement village with its own prides, a place that fought furiously to avoid being sucked in by Glasgow back in 1911. It hadn't lost its superciliousness by the time we arrived. Schoolmates from the tenements explained that Corporation houses were jerry-built, and that washing your face in hot water in the morning weakened you. Hot baths softened the spine too, an established scientific fact.

This was defensive or inverted snobbery, also common in this savagely egalitarian city, and I had a lot of sympathy with it, especially as I had fallen wildly in love at the age of ten with a lassie who lived up a close in Shettleston Road and everything connected with her had to be totally perfect. It didn't last, if you're interested.

"Ah, youth was the drouth in the sooth o' the mooth . . ."

Anyway, I would never have felt socially superior to the cliff-dwellers because I am of course your archetypal Glasgow intellectual, living spiritually outside and beyond the class or snob-scruff system. So it's only natural that when I married and found a place to live in the West End, I felt absolutely furtive. Lord Carmichael, who was in my class at Eastbank Academy, had the same experience, the unshakeable suspicion that he wasn't *entitled* to live in the West End and that his base origins would be blazingly obvious to the first-class citizens around him, that he would be ostracised on sight and even deported.

The feeling wore off when I realised that there were some genuine scruff in the West End. We briefly shared a flat, and the kitchen and bathroom, with a couple whom we suspected of boiling nappies and curry simultaneously in the same dish. Still, when we moved to a tenement flat of our own, my brief epic with that girl in Shettleston Road had cured me of any shame. Anyway, it was nearly high class with a main door and a basement, or Garden Flat, downstairs, and not one but two toilets as well as a bathroom.

But see scruff? In the terrace house across the street was a very extended Irish family with numberless weans as well as adults of two generations whose exact relationships weren't worth trying to work out. I am not joking, the only food ever seen going into the house was hundredweight bags of potatoes delivered by lorry, and from time to time one or other of the tiny tots would be seen climbing out of the open first-floor window and crawling along the sill. We gave up rushing across to knock the door and scream a warning. The tribal group clearly took the view that one kid more or less couldn't matter a lot. Or maybe the children were immune to severe impact through repeated exposure to it.

But people of Irish origin, like my own forebears, shouldn't be allowed into Glasgow to lower the tone.

I did, actually. The very nice lady upstairs came to the door to tell my wife she had locked herself out and wondered if the workman in our house could help. The workman was I, on a ladder in the uncurtained front room doing something of an artisan nature in paint-spattered rags. The lady was shattered with embarrassment at the discovery. But I did get her door open for her, so she probably thinks till this day that her first assumption was spot on. Behind the debonair owner-occupier facade, a scruff, born with a cold chisel in his hand.

In the same scruffy duds, which included a red shirt, a horrible red shirt received as a gift and instantly demoted to dungaree status, I answered the door to another lady recruiting or collecting for the local Unionist Association, whose committee, she assured me, really understood what political realities were about. I suggested diffidently that I had some knowledge of political realities. She didn't quite scoff, but she did say, "Yes, I mean, it's one thing for people like you or me to have some ideas, but they're experienced businessmen, it's not the same thing. Or," she added, a wee bit white at the nostrils, "does your shirt tell your politics?"

"No, not really." I was really very gentle, I have an evil pleasure in these encounters. "I have a blue one for painting in the basement."

I don't know who won that one, but I know she knew a scruff when she saw one.

But my most direct encounter with the upstairs-downstairs syndrome was during that brief romantic encounter in Shettleston, when one of the girl's friends and neighbours had some philosophical disagreement with me, and ended it with a haughty toss of the curls and, "I should know what to expect, with somebody who's got a bit of string in his sand-shoe instead of a lace."

I was staggered at the naked discourtesy, the crudity of the snobbery. It broke all the rules of civilised society. The accomplished snob never says a thing like that, certainly not in Glasgow.

He merely *thinks* it. And how richly satisfying that is.

Mine eyes have seen the glory of the coming . . .

ENCOUNTERS

Billy Connolly

I LEARNED THIS tune from a fellow called Harry Campbell, who went to banjo lessons wi' me when he was about seventy, and he was tryin' to take it up as a hobby. But he had been a miner, and his fingers were very stiff, and he didn't quite make it, so he stopped the lessons after a couple of weeks. I didn't see him again for a couple of years, and then one night I went for a drink, as was my wont of an evening, and I went to Anderston, down at the dockside. Anderston is a quaint fishing village on the Clyde.

I was having a pint when I heard the plinkaplink of a banjo noise fae the lounge, and I thought, "Aw haw?", and took a wee look in. And there was the cabaret—Harry Campbell, sittin' wi' his banjo, in the spotlight, and he was playing —and I seriously thought he was a comedy turn because of the things he was doin'.

"Ah ha ha ha, look at that, that's magic, innit ha ha ha . . ." and discovered I was the only one that was laughing. And there were a coupla hard cases, friends of his, there at the front, wi' the broken noses.

"Who he? Who him? Get the body, bring 'is body doon here!"

I was terrified, because they're rough doon there. I mean, they don't do simple things like punching you on the nose or anything like that, they wait till you go for chips and they ambush you.

Tell you a wee story about that area. There was a guy called Willie McQuade, a friend of mine, and he was coming home one night, drunk. He had a fish supper in one hand and a bottle of Irn Bru in his pocket, like a gunfighter. Staggering through Anderston, he came round a corner, eating his chips, and he saw four enormous hard men beating up a wee man in the street. Four gorillas, bootin' him.

"Ooo ya. Ooo ya. Haud him up, ah want tae pit the heid on um!"

So Willie saw this, and he shouted, "Aw hey, hey, hey, at's terrible, at." That's Gaelic for, "Here, just a minute chaps, that's a bit thick."

So the four gorillas looks up.

"Who's that? Who's that shoutin'?"

"That's a liberty, gie's a brek, that's terrible, that."

"Get um!"

So these four monsters came charging up the street, Ooya, gaunty kill you— their knuckles a' blood wi' draggin' them alang behind them, Gonny kill yooooo.

So Willie said, "Aye, awright," and threw his fish supper away. And a dug ran away wi' it. So there was nae goin' back, it was like a cowboy picture. "Okay, come on!"

So they came charging up Aooya, so he pulled the Irn Bru out his pocket, smashed it aff the wa' and was left wi' the cork. It was like John Wayne and the empty gun. He threw the cork, and got off his mark.

GLASGOW SONNET

Carl MacDougall

Thanks a lot son; it's nice tae be nice
intit. That's whit Ah always say:
Ah'm no tappin mind, it's jist that the day
Ah'm a bit short an wonnered if you'd the price
o a cup of tea and meybe somethin fur a slice
o breid, eh? Thanks. Ah'm jist on ma wey
doon tae Watterloo Street; they pey
me oot there. Some folk widnae think twice
aboot askin fur money in the street. No me.
Definately not. Naw, ma faither wis wan
o they Black an Tans that fought in the Free
State. Aye they fun him deid wi a gun
in Edinburgh. He wis a strict man, meybe a wee
bit too strict sometimes. Well, God bless ye son.

Out in the beautiful twilight

GLASGOW SONNET

Carl MacDougall

Naw but. It's aa very well tae talk, but ye feel
rotten when the screw slams yon big door on
your face, an aa you'll hear is: "Right then son,
here's your purridge." Ah mean, if you steal
somethin fur a drink and then the bogies wheel
ye oot wance you've had it, or you'll maybe pawn
somethin fur a drink, an then the money's gone;
the jile's aa there is, pal. See; if you deal
in that gemme, you'll get caught, and shoved in
wi two bampots that's daft as yoursel. One
thing ah mind, wis getting the jile wi this yin
they ca'd "Radio Luxemburg" cause he'd done
twu hunner an eight meters. An him wantin a pin
tae pick the lock wi! Christ! It wisnae fun.

THE VIEW FROM THE BENCH

Andrew Lothian

WHAT'S THE BEST way to come into Glasgow? It could be down the valley of the Clyde, through the rich farmlands of Lanarkshire, or along the motorway from Edinburgh, glancing over one shoulder at the gasometers, over the other at HM Prison, Barlinnie, and ending up in the old town, surrounded by all the comforts of the Saltmarket. It could be round by the Campsies, through the trim villages of commuter country to douce Anniesland and the elegances of Great Western Road; or from the West, contemplating the beauties of and cursing the traffic on, the Bonnie Banks of Loch Lomond, or else pondering the nuclear prospects and high rateable values of Rhu and Helensburgh.

Such a choice alerts one to the place's variousness, but the simplest thing might be to step from the train at Queen Street and to go out and brave the civic pomp and statuesque glories of George Square. Better still, one could be born in Glasgow and just not leave, as many people have done and still do.

I regret that I was not born in Glasgow, although I spent my formative years there, exploring the possibilities of Newlands. As an involuntary exile from Stirling, to me Glasgow came to represent the Good Place; from vanished Buchanan Street Station after a family journey smelling of BR fluff and the *Picture Post*, it was downhill all the way, pausing at the pleasures of the Stamp Shop, to Rowan's for a regulation grey school shirt, then west past trams and trace-horses to the pantomime and the gentle foolery of Alec Finlay or the disturbingly grotesque sophistication of Jack Radcliffe.

Later I often visited Glasgow with friends on pleasure bent. Our appetites were various. It could be to Ibrox for the Police Sports; to the Pavilion, for the lengths to which Lex McLean would go to get a dirty laugh while staying clean; to the cinema to see more of Brigitte Bardot than we were likely to at home; or even to play tennis with nice girls from Broomlee ("Broomielaw, more like," said my father darkly. He had an office in St Vincent Street).

I mention this collection of experiences to show that, while I live in Glasgow now, I recognise that I can never be a Glaswegian; that is a distinction conferred by a lucky accident of birth. Like a friend of mine who lived in Perth and believed that professional boxing existed only on the radio ("inter-round summaries by Barrington Dalby"), my experience of Glasgow is that of the idealistic outsider, who likes to think that the whole place is a work of the imagination, created to give pleasure; where the banal and the bizarre rest their arms comfortably round one another's shoulders.

In the Folk Song Club in Cathedral Street, for example, a place poor in decor but not in spirit, I heard the matter-of-fact announcement, "If anybody's wanting

Showing the flag, and several others

guitar lessons they should put their names down soon because Bert's away for the winter to Morocco".

Or take the following: A man who had been seen by a passing beat policeman at 2 a.m. standing on the roof of a warehouse pulling ineffectually at a wire grating, did not give himself up easily. In the end it took four constables and the crew (and ladders) of a fire engine to get him down. None of those involved seemed to bear him any ill-will, either at the time or when they came to give evidence in Court.

Apart from suggesting that he was the unfortunate victim of a manifest misunderstanding, the accused too was without rancour. The reason he had been up there, he said, was that while walking a girl home from the disco earlier that night, he had remembered that he had passed the self-same building some two weeks before. On that occasion, in a moment of pique, he had thrown on to the roof a diamond engagement ring returned to him that night by his ex-fiancée following a row about some sheets.

Having safely delivered his new friend, he had made his way back to the warehouse and had climbed a drainpipe, stepped on to the roof and begun to search to see if the missing ring was still there. When he became aware of the officer's torch shining on him, he realised that his situation was likely to be misinterpreted and in his own words, "just panicked and wouldn't come down".

This lively account proved unacceptable to the Court, but it did show something of the Glasgow character at its best. Cheerful, optimistic and imaginative, the accused clearly felt that others would readily share in his acceptance of this remarkable turn of events. Normally, no doubt, he would have just slipped off; forced to give an explanation, he made sure that his tale was worth the telling.

To leave the scene of a crime abruptly when discovered, incidentally, is not necessarily thought to be evidence of guilt; one Glasgow Sheriff observed some years ago that it was the inalienable right of every Glaswegian who saw the police coming to get off his mark.

It seems to me paradoxical that the name of Glasgow should at one and the same time stand for what is best and worst in human achievement. The label "Clyde-built" was a guarantee of excellence; the claim to be the Second City of the Empire was no vain boast. All the same, the name of the city did become a by-word, a shorthand expression for violence, squalor and deprivation.

One reason for this confusion in the popular mind may be that while Glasgow has been well served by what it produced, be it the great ships of the Clyde or the great paintings of the Glasgow Boys, it has often been ill served by those who have chosen to write about it. *No Mean City* is the notorious example, of course, and it remains in print, spreading the despondent view of the city among the unwary and the unknowing, but its authors have not been the only ones to treat Glasgow as if it dwelt at the heart of some Blakean apocalypse.

It may be that timid people are attracted by violent themes. There is more than one sort of sentimentality. It seems to me, however, that not just a corrective, but in fact a more recognisable rendering of the spirit of the place is to be found in such more charitable works as George Friel's *Mr Alfred M.A.*, Alan Spence's *The Colours They are Fine,* and Cliff Hanley's *Dancing in the Streets.*

A serious blow at the Walk

This is not to deny the city has its faults. Although not as smug as Aberdeen or as mean as Edinburgh, Glasgow does have the melancholy distinction of being a centre of institutionalised religious bigotry. The continuing mindless sectarianism of young football supporters may be little more than an excuse for verbal and actual violence, but their pitiful attachment to the club of their preference is as noxious as their assumption that in their colours and *en masse*, the streets are theirs.

Another, more recent curse which particularly involves the young is the spread of the drug heroin. This is not a problem for Glasgow alone, but inasmuch as it is particularly the drug of the unintelligent and the inadequate, the city has its share.

Glasgow is fortunate of course in having what every city aspiring to greatness must, that is to say a river running through the middle. It is not enough just to be *on* a river. The presence of water as a dividing line brings out something special in the citizens, so that those on one side can have the pleasure of regarding those on the other as distinctly transpontine.

Whether the achievements of each side are characteristic of anything in particular is debatable; the North can boast a Cathedral, Kelvingrove Park and the cosmopolitan exuberance of Byres Road, while the South can point to the splendours of the Pollok Estate, Hampden Park, the brilliant Citizens' Theatre, where the highest standards of artistic excellence have not succeeded in putting off the paying customers, and the graceful residential certainties of Pollokshields.

Fortunate Glaswegians can of course, and do, cross and recross the river in search of fun; they can go down it in a boat. The story of the man who spends his holidays at "Dead Slow" on the Clyde may be true, but it is usually recognised that a better time is to be had in Rothesay, Dunoon or Millport.

So what would we recommend to the visitor to the city? There are the great obviousnesses, of course; the Burrell, the Barras and the Botanics; Salvador Dali at Kelvingrove and Whistler at the Hunterian. I'd add the People's Palace, the Tron Theatre club and naturally, what some people consider to be a mixture of the two, the Sheriff Court in Ingram Street. One lawyer there told me recently that he had been consulted by a man charged with offences involving a dubious approach to the buying and selling of second-hand furniture. The charges were not of particular gravity, but the lawyer considered it necessary to find out about the man's background.

"Tell me about yourself," he said, "age, family, address—what do you call yourself?"

"Well, sir," was the reply, "as far as the state's concerned I just don't exist. I haven't got an insurance number, if that's what you call it, and since my granny died I haven't really been keeping up the books and that."

"I'll have to call you something, though," his legal adviser explained.

The man thought a bit, then his face brightened. "How about a manoeuverer?" he said.

THE HYPE

Robin Hall

MY LOVE AFFAIR with Glasgow patter and *Ra Barras* (the two go hand in hand, I think) began just after the War, when I was ten. Admittedly, these days, you get a fair amount of the flim-flam boys from "Dahn Saath" but there's still an eloquent sufficiency of Glesca patter, at its best, to be heard down Calton way at the weekend.

Mind you, the trader who stands out most in my memory does, in fact, go back to my childhood. He is, or was, a wee man with a bunnet, a Tommy Morgan voice and a supply of the very first, post-war, elasticated gents' braces . . . "Gether roon', gether roon' an' get yur elasticated galluses here! No even Copeland and Lye's've goat them in yet! *(!!Twang!!)* No only dae these galluses haud up your winners an' losers, but therr rerr fur swattin' blueboatles when yu'r sittin' in ra cludgie oan a warm sunny day! *(!!Twang!!)* In fact these galluses ur so deadly accurate that ye'll start runnin' oot o' blueboatles! *(!!Twang!!)* But, never fear chinas. Wae a coupla oors' practice ye'll get that good ye'll be able tae only stun the wee buggers, pit them in a matchboax and let them oot fur yur next session in ra cludgie! C'moan up and get yur elasticated galluses! *(!!Twang!!)*"

The wee man also had a line in balloons. Certainly the first I'd ever clapped eyes on: "Ye've nae conception a the use o' ma balloons. Yase ma balloons an' ye'll huv nae conception!"

He sold them three for three-ha' pence.

Nothing but the best

BAREFOOT BEAUTY

Bartholomew Faujas St Fond

I WAS GREATLY astonished, in a climate so cold and moist as that of Glasgow, to see the greater part of the lower class of women, and even many of those in easy circumstances, going about with bare feet and bare heads, their bodies covered only with a bodice, petticoat and a cloak of red stuff, which descends to the middle of their legs; their fine long hair hanging down without any other ornament than a simple curved comb to keep back what would otherwise fall over their faces.

This garb of the females, quite simple as it is, is not without grace, and since nothing impedes their movements, they have an elegance and agility in their gait so much the more striking, as they are in general tall, well made, and of a charming figure. They have a bright complexion, and very white teeth. It is not to be inferred, because they walk bare-legged, that they are neglectful of cleanliness; for it appears that they wash frequently, and with equal facility, both their feet and their hands . . .

The vicinity of the mountains attracts a considerable number of Highlanders to this city. Their antique costume, much resembling that of the Roman soldiers, forms a remarkable contrast with the dress of the women and the other inhabitants . . . In the environs of Glasgow a considerable number of mines yield coal of excellent quality. These make manufacturers and commerce to prosper; and thereby increase the happiness of the inhabitants.

Travels in England and Scotland

Water nymph

DIGGING IN

Bet Low

NOT BEING ONE of those who, bitten early by the travel bug, continues to extol the virtues of foreign travel, I have always preferred to stay put in one place for a

The Mackintosh motif of Glasgow School of Art

reasonable length of time, and it's never been the means of getting there but the arrival, the feeling of being there, that has always mattered most.

I think the tall tales of my father's travels round the world (well, more or less) and of his twenty very odd years in India, would have been reason enough to turn me off for life. (I can't stand hot climates, and I still don't like elephants.) And after three years of daily bus and desperately slow train trips to Glasgow during wartime, blackout and all, I knew I'd no intention of being a commuter one single day longer. AND, as there seemed little prospect of establishing a St Ives anywhere between Gourock and the Cloch Lighthouse, I plumped for staying in Glasgow.

That was in 1945! And any moment now it'll be 1985 and that means I'll have been here for all of forty years! (Well, I said I liked to stay put for a reasonable length of time.)

But go back to the Forties. For it's those years I always recall with affection (O Nostalgia, Nostalgia) and recently they were brought vividly to life again, by having to look through—for the first time in those forty years—old folios of drawings of Glasgow people and places for an exhibition so entitled.

Anyway, I'd just left Art School with a special wartime Diploma in Drawing and Painting. The three years there had been very exciting. Each morning, from the moment I staggered out of the dirty old steam train at Central Station, I felt the thrill of being in the city, big, noisy and very black . . . how black the buildings were . . . black soot flakes fell from the station roof or black raindrops if it had been raining.

With the shriek of the engine in my ears, I would rush from the station, and after the usual moment or two of sheer panic (the delight and panic always went together) would hurry as fast as my legs would carry me, up Hope Street, along Sauchiehall Street, up Dalhousie Street (or up the slower incline of Renfrew Street if there was snow or ice about) and home at last, through the doors of that great Mackintosh building, the Glasgow School of Art.

I took to the building from the moment I first saw it. I thought it was great. I loved everything about it, the studios, the dark wood, the ironwork, the library, and maybe especially the Hen Run, that glass-sided corridor high up in the building, which provided endless subjects for drawing with its panoramic views over the roofs of the city.

It must also have been being young, being in the company of similarly interested people, beginning to learn to paint, just beginning, making a start in life that made everything seem so good, so alive, in the middle of the war that was on.

We were short on staff, so some subjects like ceramics were out; short on food, clothes and money, though we didn't seem to need very much. For extra cash, we'd do extra firewatching, for which we were paid 3/6d per night. (We all knew our chances and the Mackintosh's were slim, if firebombs really were to fall on us.) This handsome sum was more than enough for a hearty wartime breakfast in Ma Brown's smokeroom—the other place we practically lived in. And the change left over, believe it or not, added to the pennies saved by not taking the tram, secured our daily fags, Woodbines, coffin nails, from the girl in the kiosk across the road, as everyone who was anyone (we thought) smoked, in those dark, bad old days. Later on, as even Woodbines were hard to come by, we had to do with Pasha—a cigarette so vile tasting and smelling that no one who had to smoke them could ever possibly forget.

There were so few students compared with now, that in our final years, each of us could select and have a studio exclusively, and have complete freedom to work in the evenings or weekends or any time at all. There were no grants (some students took night jobs on newspapers and suchlike to help pay their fees and materials), no travelling scholarships, no great technical advances or equipment and no decent meals. Today's students would no doubt throw up (or throw up their hands) in horror at the thought of such solitary deprivation . . . but for me, nothing could be better than the freedom, quiet, space, and ability to be on my own whenever I wished. These were the days . . . I'm very glad I was there at that time.

However, afterwards, out and on my own (for I no more thought to teach than fly) a studio had to be found and paid for somehow, as that was regarded by all who

Eardley the Great

were serious about painting as essential. In those days, there were still a good number of artists' studios in the town, as well as photographers' studios, and other suitable attic properties. You can still see some of them (best from the top of a bus) in Bath Street, West Regent Street and St Vincent Street, and further afield in

Townhead and Garscube Road there were fine ones too; but they have all been demolished. Nowadays, few young artists seem to want to work quietly on their own . . . they all appear to work in communes.

Anyway, rooms were found, the differences were few, the similarities numerous—like being totally empty, brown, sooty, and perishingly cold. Twelve shillings and sixpence was about the average weekly rent, though, if one were lucky, a smaller, cleaner attic room in a lodging house might be had for ten shillings a week. I know, for I stayed in one in Renfrew Street. Though warned that the landlady was very strict (not to say nuts) I was dismayed to find myself locked out just after 11 pm on my very first night. After much hammering at the front door, the bolts and chains were removed, and I was allowed in, on the clear understanding that I must pack and leave next morning. There was no answer to that. So much for my ten bob. No rent tribunal in those days.

Some time later on, I moved into a much bigger freezing room in Sauchiehall Street—so cold I wore a coat, scarf and gloves most of the time (don't forget, this was the awful winter of 1946-47). It looked straight over to what was then the last detached house in Sauchiehall Street, which though still being used as a wartime refugee centre, had also become the home of Unity Theatre. The days and evenings spent there were magical ones for me. Conversations would go on until the small hours in the company of actors, writers, poets and painters from all over Britain and Europe. We even had a brilliant young German nuclear physicist, singers in Gaelic from Lewis, and a Russian sailor who carved little wooden animals, in the company.

There was work to be had too—stage sets to be designed and painted, posters and costumes made, and best of all, there were lots of willing sitters to draw and paint. Some of these paintings were exhibited in London in the Galeria Appolinaire, as the "The Gorbals Story" was being staged in London.

Glasgow seemed to abound in clubs and groups then. I frequented the Unity, the New Art Club at Blythswood Square, the Iona Community House in Clyde Street—all of which held regular exhibitions of paintings—the Press Club (very dull and dark), and later there was "The Good Companions" and many more. The Clyde Group was a typical group of that time, with a Manifesto stating its aims and objectives. There was a lot of that about then . . . many seemed to feel it very necessary to make positive statements and commitments. The Clyde Group believed, among other things, in "taking Art to the People", so exhibitions were often lugged to, and poetry readings held in, distant lands like Househillwood and the Calton for sometimes only one-night stands in the community centres there. I can't say I ever remember a crowd. This was our never-to-be-forgotten early missionary work, preaching to the lucky or unlucky few.

As well as the portraits and sketches made in the studio, there was the great "outdoors". The worst of the old dark crumbling tenements both attracted and repelled, with their barred windows and turrets like prisons, and evil-smelling closes—who could wish to live in them? But they were there to be drawn, all round Gorbals, Rottenrow, Townhead, Cowcaddens, the Barrows, Paddy's Market.

But it was more invigorating (i.e. freezing) of a winter's day, to sit and draw up by the Canal where there were the Puffers, and old grain mills and sawmills, and if you climbed up the Cuddy's Park (Pinkston) the views over Glasgow could keep you busy forever.

It was just possible for the air to be fresh up there, but if the wind changed, and it usually did, great gusts of sulphuric smoke would descend from Tennent's works and all but finish life on earth. And with the white steam billowing from Pinkston's giant cooling towers, and malodorous vapours issuing from the swamplands of the chemical dump at your feet, it seemed as if you had been transported back in time to wander through that far-off garden with Hieronymus Bosch.

Frames for the masterpieces of those days could be found in plentiful supply in any of the hundreds of junk shops all over the city. My favourite haunts were those of West Graham Street, Shamrock Street (packed from floor to ceiling with beautiful oil lamps) and Garscube Road, which was a real hive of activity. They cost practically nothing, and some were very fine, needing little more than a clean. A frame was usually chosen specially to suit each painting, and could be sandpapered, stained, stuccoed or stripped in a very individual way. The more I see framed work from that period, the more I prefer it to the mass-produced uniformity of today.

There were few cars in town, and the tram was the thing. How I miss them— even the tremendous din in the middle of the night as gangs of workmen laboured at repairing the rails right below my Sauchiehall Street window! Those days *everybody* travelled by tram—rich, poor, young and old. A great form of transport, none better, and if you played your cards right, you could nearly do a flitting by tram! You had to run round the front to the driver's side when it was stationary, clutching or dragging your table, easel or settee, and ask him very nicely to take it on board beside him. Maybe he would have turned down a wardrobe, but a table or chair got a lift everytime. Walking was the alternative to jumping on a tram (and you did jump on). Well-trodden routes were from St George's Cross to Charing Cross—from Wood & Selby's to R. Sheldon Bamber's.

Now one whole side of the street has vanished and traffic rushes through the shades of the old Grand Hotel. There were fascinating grocers and bakers round Gorbals Cross, and shops galore in Cowcaddens selling everything you could possibly need from fish, poultry and meat to clothes, shoes and ironmongery. It used to be packed on a Saturday, from the very young in shawls, to the very old in theirs—the Shawlies.

This was the area that attracted me most—I especially liked going down Renfrew Street from Art School, through Queen's Arcade with its glass ironwork, and returning later via the little lane with its book and junk shops into Cambridge Street, across and up Buccleuch Street where someone once had a studio . . .

Now, forty years on, all is honey-coloured stonework and light, and the blackness has been banished . . . but so too have some of the deep, rich glowing colours. If only one could pick and choose . . . or is it that all is for the best in this best of all possible worlds?

However, these forty years on, and not much wiser, one views Glasgow with a less innocent eye. Perhaps, after all, Glasgow's Miles Better?

BALLADE

Ebenezer McIlwham

There was yince a Kate McCurdy, a sonsie-lukkin' burdie
Was the dochter o' a bowly-leggit lairdie
She was smit by Cupid's arra when she trippit ower a barra
And the gairdner picked her up and gi'ed her bairdie

Will ye mairry me ma fair yin, said the reckless proletarian
And she swooned a wee, as was the auld-time fashion
As he felt the lassie reelin', the gairdner's bluid was bealin'
So he stoopit ower and stole anither ration

Michty me, she cried, we're loony, and ah'm burstin' oot ma goonie
Wha'd ha' thocht a wee bit gairdner had sic courage?
And ah ken ah should be greetin', for ma oxters fair are sweitin'
And ma braith is comin' oot like lumpy purridge

Faur awa' we baith maun trauchle, for altho' ah'm jist a bauchle
Yet ah fancy you quite strangly, cried the laddie.
And for a' ah've had a duffy, still ah ken ah'm ower scruffy
Tae be smiled on by your bowly-leggit Daddy.

You're no kiddin, said the burdie, shooglin' wan weel-shapit hurdie
It's the high jump if he fin's you've gi'ed me bairdie
For ah'm promised tae McCuish, a knicht wha's bluid is bluish
And nae man will thwart the wishes o' the lairdie

Noo the laird blew aff his thatch, he saw the lassie's face a'scratchy
And jaloused the cause, to his severe displeesure
When he glimped her torn peenie, he smashed a pile o' cheeny
And he tummled ower his wulkies for guid meesure

Loack her up, the lairdie shriekit, see that a' the doors are steikit
And we'll hunt the gairdner doon wi' wally dugs
We will chase him sair ferfochen frae Drumry tae Auchenlochan
And we'll hing him frae the yairdairm by his lugs

But the laddie had gaen unnerground and faith it was nae wunner
For he didnae want his lugs peened tae a wa'
His wee barra he was shovin' ower the Clyde and doon tae Govan
Whaur his auntie steyed, his uncle tae and a'

A' this time young Kate McCurdy had got up frae aff her hurdy
And disguisit as a puir wee peasant scrubber
She had loupit through a transom and she cried a passin' hansom
Sayin' "Govan, quick, or else we're in the grubber."

Fair and fast the cabbie whuppit, aiblins doon the street and up it
Sayin', Ah will get ye safely ower, ma hen.
And the boatman didnae tarry as he scooshed the Govan Farry
Till young Katie raxed the gairdner's but-and-ben

Then young love was brocht thegither as they cuddled yin anither
And he asked her "Wull ye?" and she whispered "Yes."
And he gi'ed the lass a hunker far ayont abune the bunker
And they gropit through the dim-lit lobby press

Here should end our joyfu' saga as she filled his pipe wi' shag, a
Rich tobauca wham a workin' man tak's tint
But she'd hardly gi'ed it to him when the rattlin' o' a brougham
Telt them baith the fremit laird was close ahint

"Post that nyuck tae the West Indie, either that or oot the windae,"
Said the laird, "Ah canny thole him in ma sicht."
And his men-at-airms, richt merry, for they'd kissed the Govan Ferry
Flang the gairdner intae Govan's plumbless nicht.

"Brick her up," the faither shreikit, "tae a peasant she's been cleekit.
Her dishonour maun be hidden frae the warl."
So they bashed awa' wi trowels while the puir young lassie's bowels
Moved wi' love for her defenestrated carl.

Ye maun ken that in yon ages, prolies worked for fear, no' wages
And the lairdies whiles wad brick folk up tae stey
They wad hardly tak' the road withoot a brickie's lorry-load
For fear they took the notion on the wey.

So the lairdie, quite frenetic, sealed his dochter up hermetic
Deif tae a' her cries for mercy and remede
But when efter he'd depertit, oh, then up the gairdner stertit
For the bold young lusty laddie wisnae deid.

For his auntie kept some kye, and a soo or twa forbye
Wha cauld fertilise an acre while ye waitit
And as doon tae earth he dreept, a convenient steamin' heap
His precipitate descent deceleratit

Up the rone-pipe sune he sclimmed, tho' his een we glaur were dimmed
And he pu'd the bricks oot brawly, twa by twa
She was waitin' for him shairly and he had the lassie fairly
Up agin her faither's haun-constructed wa'

In the lairdie's big stane castle there's a dolefu' annual hassle
When they mourn the shamefu' death o' puir young Kate
They ken naethin' o' the shovin' in that wee brick press in Govan
And the gairdner and his lass don't gi'e a haet.

ONLY DIAMONDS ARE FOREVER

(A Phyliss Marlowe Story)

Liz Lochhead

A MEMORY OF Glasgow in the Sixties. (Which didn't stop till 1973 . . .)

The letters lying there on the mat didn't exactly look as though if I didn't open them the world would stop.

I picked them up. I turned them over, squinting through the bloodshot marblings of my hangover and the tangled remains of last night's Twiggy eyelashes. It was back in sixty-six. Those days the world was a more innocent place.

I fanned out the fistful of manilla in my mitt. As I had thought. Zilch. A final demand from the Gas Board and a threat from Glasgow Public Libraries if I didn't return *The Maltese Falcon* and pay my seventeen-and-six fine they'd permanently withdraw my ticket and cut my left hand off. And what was this? I swallowed. I swallowed again. An appointment card, report today, today at two-thirty, the Brook Clinic, a discreet logo and an address, a classy address in the city's ritzy West End.

I showered, shaved—shaved my legs—like I said this was back in sixty-six, the world was a more innocent place, those days no one accused you of anti-feminism if you were caught with a tube of Immac. I sniffed. I showered again.

I emerged from the bathroom a half an hour later in a cloud of Amplex Aerosol avalanched in Boots' 365 Talcum. The place looked like the ski-slopes at Chamonix.

I shimmied shivering to the bedsit, slotted another shilling into the gas fire and reached for the knob on the third drawer of the tallboy. I knew exactly what I was looking for, they had to be here somewhere—the one and only pair of knickers left uncontaminated in that disastrous load at the launderette, the stuff that had got washed along with that bargain-price bright-pink non-fast Indiancotton mini-skirt from C & A. Some bargain, huh? These days I peeked out at the world through unevenly rose-tinted underwear.

I found them at last. Virgin white as the day they crossed the counter at Galls. I slid them on. Two-thirty, huh? I showered again.

Two-twenty-five found me on the steps of a slightly crumbling mansion in what the Estate Agents would call a highly desirable residential area. A simple brass plaque spelt out Brook Advisory Clinic. The whole place screamed Anonymity.

I pressed the bell. The door creaked open a couple of inches.

"Yes?" said a voice more frosted than the glass-panels on the door. I showed her my card.

"Two-thirty," I barked.

She barked back, the door slid open wide enough for me to enter and I found myself in a roomful of dames all with rigor mortis of the third-finger-of-the-left-hand. Engagement rings. Woolworth's engagement rings, each a lump of glass as big as the Ritz. There was more imitation ice than in *The Ancient Mariner*, more gilt than in a pyschiatrist's office, more rolled gold than in Acapulco.

Tonight these dames were going to have greener fingers than Percy Thrower.

Each broad had a Tame Boyfriend with her, like a poodle on a lead. All you could see of any of them was a pair of very pink ears sticking out behind old copies of the *Woman's Own*. Nobody in the place looked exactly relaxed.

Lochhead sings the Blues

I sat down. Dame opposite was wearing laddered black Beatle nylons—Jesus, nobody had worn Beatle nylons since sixty-four for Chrissakes—she looked like some George Square wino's version of a vision from the DTs. She was reading *The Uses of Literacy*. Maybe she did have an honours degree in sociology, but she certainly was sixpence short in the shilling when it came to dress-sense. Still, somebody loved her. Otherwise she wouldn't be here. I slid my eyes over the gent she had accessorising her. Below magazine-level at any rate he was not painful to look at.

Over in the corner behind a gigantic desk sat this old bird who looked as though she had been there since Marie Stopes was pre-pubescent.

"Next!" she plainsonged and fixed me with an oldfashioned look from behind her lorgnette.

I sidled over. "Name," she stated.

"Marlowe," I quipped. "Marlowe with an 'e'. Phyliss Marlowe. 'Ph' for Phellatio, 'Y' for Yesplease, 'L' for Love, 'L' for Leather, 'I' for Intercourse, 'S' for . . ."

She looked at me as though I had said a dirty word.

"In there," she said, "remove tights and pants, lie up on that table. Doctor will be here to examine you directly." She pronounced it like Doktor with a "k". I gulped. I must pull myself together. I loosened my waistband and pulled myself together.

I found myself in a rough cubicle with a torn curtain hanging to approximately knee-height. Through this, various bits of anonymous female gooseflesh and, in the ringing tones of a Roedean Gymnmistress, Doktor's voice interrogating the bimbo-next-door about the ins-and-outs of her sexlife. The whole place was about as private as Grand Central Station on Glasgow Fair Saturday.

Five minutes later found me flinching and clenching, biting into the black vinyl of the couch as cold steel penetrated. I spat out a curse.

Ten minutes after that—I sat in triumph, six precious months supply of the pill in my grasp.

Doktor wagged a metronome finger at me.

"You must take for twenty-one days religiously, stop for seven, always begin on the same day of the week, got it? Now, what do you do?"

"I'm a student at Jordanhill College doing Fribble," I riposted.

She gave me a look, I returned it, she slammed it back, I caught it neatly, spun round and delivered a deft backward glance over my left shoulder.

Back in the waiting room it had gotten twice as crowded. Obviously there was a future in this business, they'd hit a nerve somewhere.

Then I saw him. Shoulder-length blond hair, embroidered cheese-cloth shirt, single strand of beads—I mean, beads but *tasteful*—a sensual hint of hash and patchouli, and midnight blue denim stretched taut then flaring over the longest, leanest bass-guitarist's thighs in Glasgow. Like, this guys loons had *style*. I'd loved him for as long as I could remember. I'd have known him anywhere.

"Haw, thingmy," he jack-knifed to his feet. "Whit urr you daeing here?"

"I might ask you the same question."

His Adam's apple slid up and down his throat like the lift in the Red Road Flats oughta, but don't.

"Hey, listen doll, great to see you, oh aye. Hiv tae git you roon tae wir new flat in Wilton Street, listen to a few albums, smoke a few joints, Fat Freddy's got some Moroccan in, really good stuff . . . toodle-oo!" he gabbled.

I looked over his shoulder. Coming towards him, big smile freezing fast, was this Julie Christie lookalike in Fringed Suede.

I smiled a lopsided smile. "So long Blue-Eyes, see you around."

Outside it was still raining. On my way through Kelvingrove Park I flipped my once-precious packet into a wastebasket and walked on.

Last I saw, a couple of hand-in-hand schoolkids had fished them out and were avidly reading the instruction leaflet. Probably disappointed to find it wasn't twenty-one tabs of acid. Sex is wasted on the young.

Back in the bedsit, I spooned bitter instant into my Union-Jack-I'm-Backing-Britain mug—this was sixty-six, the world was a more innocent place—and sighed. I guessed I'd just have to swallow it strong and hot and black and bitter, I'd run clean out of Marvel. I ripped the cellophane off another packet of chocolate digestives.

RANGERS' NEW SIGNING

Tom Leonard

(ALEX *enters brandishing a copy of the* Evening Times.)

Alex: Heh Wullie! Rangers huv signed the Pope!

Wullie: Whut?

Alex: Rangers huv signed the Pope! It's oan the back page! Listen tay this. (*Reads*) Ibrox supremo Jock Wallace silenced his critics this morning when he emerged from behind closed doors to announce that Glasgow Rangers have signed the head of the Roman Catholic Church, His Holiness Pope John Paul the Second. Denying that the signing had any religious significance, Mr Wallace said that the Pontiff's gritty tackling, his intelligent running off the ball, and his flair for the unexpected box-to-box defensive break, had been one of the most closely guarded Vatican secrets of post-war years. For his part, the Pope was reported to be "over the moon" at the speed with which the hush-hush deal had been clinched. The Papal jet is expected to fly out from Rome this evening in time for the Holy Father to take the field in tomorrow's all-important tussle with Kilmarnock at Rugby Park.

A day tripper at Bellahouston

Wullie: Whut huv they signed the Pope fur? When did *he* last kick a baw? He's ancient!

Alex: Naw, it's good tay huv an auld heid in the defence, Wullie. Look at Ronnie Simpson wi Celtic. Ah think they'll use the Pope as a sub.

Wullie: Yi canny bring the Pope oan as a sub—yi'd huv tay kerry him oan in a chair!

Alex: He'll be wearing the red-white-and-blue, Wullie. There's naibdy gets kerried aboot in a chair wearing the red-white-and-blue.

Wullie: Aye right enough. Dae yi think he'll turn?

Alex: The Pope?

Wullie: Aye.

Alex: Naw—no right away anyway. He'll no turn afore the Kilmarnock gemme, it widny look right. It'd look as if Rangers hud pit the pressure oan him.

Wullie: Spoil the effect, aye. They'd need tay go lookin fur another wan. An they'll no get another Pope in a hurry!

Alex: Stull, Ah think they've the heid screwed oan. There's wan problem Rangers'll no huv wi His Holiness Pope John Paul the Second.

Wullie: What's that Alex?

Alex: At least he wullny marry a Catholic!

McPARANOIA

William McIlvanney

THE SCENE IS the compartment of a Wembley Football Special from Glasgow. Slumped in one of the window-seats is a man in his thirties. He is ruminatively drunk. Every so often his eyes rake the other passengers. But there's no cause for alarm. He's merely flexing his malice for London.

His mate-comes in and sits beside him.

"Aye then."

"Aye."

"Whaur i' the rest o' the boays then?" the man at the window asks.

"Faurer up the train. They've flaked oot like. The beer's a' by. It couldny last forever, eh? Only twa dizzen cans."

"Aye. Right enough."

The man at the window wipes the misted pane with his hand, peers out.

"Whaur's this we're gawn through onywey?" he asks.

"Crossmyloof."

It is the following day, as the saying is, aboard another special train going

Respect for the dead

from Euston to Wembley. The coach is incredibly crowded. People are folded against one another. It seems it will only take somebody to cough to create the first recorded case of communal rupture. But suddenly, miraculously, a man who has been sitting down shoots to his feet, his arms fully extended, and bellows, "Sc-o-o-ot-l-a-a-a-n-d!" His voice describes an enormous vocal loop, fading reluctantly like a skyrocket. He collapses back into his seat, his head rolling in terrible ecstasy, a mystical transport.

A tall Englishman hanging from a strap gives the impression that he's trying to climb up it. His laughter is a tentative question.

"Whit a fuck i' you laughin' et?" the mystic asks.

The Englishman is not laughing. His is the definitive non-laugher's expression. He is, in fact, involved in a thorough investigation of an unusual stain on the ceiling of the coach, a stain he apparently hadn't noticed before. That stain is becoming something of a passion with him.

The mystic repeats his performance several times, leaving a litter of injured ear-drums in his wake. Then suddenly he goes calm. His eyes cloud with vision.

"Penicillin!" he screams.

It isn't, it transpires, an appeal for medical attention. For he goes on.

"Taur McAdam! Steam Engines! The Big Ships! We've did the lot! The greatest wee nation ever Goad put braith in. Sc-o-o-o-t-l-a-a-a-n-d!"

He subsides again, begins to mutter. The moment is past. After the mystic's ecstasy, the chafed knees, the petty aches, all the seedy little mundanities of everyday life.

"Somebody's fartit", the ex-mystic snarls. "That wis an English fart!"

It is his final sally. Instantly, spectacularly, he passes out. *Sic gloria transit.*

At the station his body is claimed by friends. They carry him up the Wembley Way like someone who has died before the citadel is stormed but who has earned the honour of getting there nevertheless. In the car-park they cajole and slap and harangue him but he's beyond their help. They leave him behind a car and sell his ticket.

Meanwhile back at the park, the sun shines on a patch of heraldic green across which players move in complex armorial ciphers, expressing nationhood, whatever that is. Denis Law has discovered again that enthusiasm against which he hones his amazing reflexes. He is playing with a verve that suggests jackets for goalposts. Jim Baxter doesn't just beat opponents, he demeans them. There are some people with white shirts there as well. Playing nearly all of the game with ten men, the Scots massacre the English 2-1.

Later that same evening: the scene is London—all of it, it seems. Nearly every tube disgorges its statutory quota of wild faces and raucous Scots voices. Nearly every taxi at nearly every corner nearly runs down a Scotsman. London is a swirl of tartan scarves, a bob of tammies.

At a corner in Fleet Street a big man has a smaller man by the arm. "Naw," he is saying. "Luk, son. Ye huvny really a bad team. Wan or two o' yese can play a bit. Yese jist huvny that extra somethin' we seem tae ha'e." He is smiling in a kindly way.

Za' a fack?

In Blackfriars Underground Station a man who is at the head of a phalanx of nudging, grinning friends is stopping a well-dressed native to say, "Excuse me, sur. But could ye direct us tae Soho?"

In Soho itself half-a-dozen betartaned figures volley out of a narrow doorway. The small card beside the doorway reads: "Jane. Model. 3rd Floor." "Come oan, boays," one of the men is gasping. "Rin fur it!" Crippled with laughter, they make their escape as a fat woman appears in the doorway, hurling insults after them. The night absorbs the incident without explanation. Ah, sweet mystery of life.

On the train back up, a man leaning out of an open carriage-door is rescued by his mates as the train thunders towards Carlisle. Presumably, he had felt the rest of his life would be an anti-climax.

That was my first trip to Wembley. Ever since then, every second year except when I was living abroad, I've gone back—from what muddied motives I'm never sure. Maybe it's just that I think belonging to a country means acquainting yourself with all its manifestations. Certainly it is for me, and perhaps for most Scots who undertake it, a very private journey.

In my mind's ear I hear the girl who lives in the tanoi-system saying: "The train standing at Platform One is the Wembley Football Special. This train has an Inferiority Complex Car where light traumas will be served throughout the journey. This train goes by way of Paranoia, calling at Little Dependency, National Neurosis and Ultima Thule."

Ambivalent, confused, struggling with my vast, invisible luggage, I'll be there.

THE WEDDING AT CANNISBURN

William McIlvanney

An' Jesus turned the watter intae wine.
"Hello therr!" wis the cry "Staun' back. Gi'es mine."

An' a' there took a heider intae it,
Feelin' as stane-dry as a witch's tit.
An' soomin' in the bevvy each and all
Joy flourished in the Cooperative Hall.
Baith sides wis mixin' even. Auntie Belle
Wis poundin' "Paper Roses" wi' a mell.
Then a sophisticated bricky fae *his* side
Jawed a fu' gless o' wine aboot the bride.
"Don't worry, hen," that big, suave punter said.
"It's nae great loass—a gey naïve house red."

An' Jesus turned the watter intae wine
An' polis caurs arrived et hauf-past nine.

THE SPLITTING OF IAN NICOL

Alasdair Gray

ONE DAY IAN NICOL, a riveter by trade, started to split in two down the middle. The process began as a bald patch on the back of his head. For a week he kept smearing it with hair restorer, yet it grew bigger, and the surface became curiously puckered and so unpleasant to look upon that at last he went to his doctor.

"What is it?" he asked.

"I don't know," said the doctor, "but it looks like a face, ha ha! How do you feel these days?"

"Fine. Sometimes I get a stabbing pain in my chest and stomach but only in the morning."

"Eating well?"

"Enough for two men."

The doctor thumped him all over with a stethoscope and said, "I'm going to have you X-rayed. And I may need to call in a specialist."

Over the next three weeks the bald patch grew bigger still and the suggestion of a face more clearly marked on it. Ian visited his doctor and found a specialist in the consulting room, examining X-ray plates against the light. "No doubt about it, Nicol," said the specialist, "you are splitting in two down the middle."

Ian considered this.

"This isn't usual, is it?" he asked.

"Oh, it happens more than you would suppose. Among bacteria and viruses it's quite common, though it's certainly less frequent among riveters. I suggest you come into hospital where the process can complete itself without annoyance for your wife or embarrassment to yourself. Think it over."

Ian thought it over and went into hospital where he was put into a small ward and given a nurse to attend him, for the specialist was interested in the case. As the division proceeded more specialists were called in to see what was happening. At first Ian ate and drank with a greed that appalled those who saw it. After consuming three times his normal bulk for three days on end he fell into a coma which lasted till the split was complete. Gradually the lobes of his brain separated and a bone shutter formed between them. The face on the back of his head grew eyelashes and a jaw. What seemed at first a cancer of the heart became another heart. Convulsively the spine doubled itself. In a puzzled way the specialists charted the stages of the process and discussed the case. A German consultant said that life was freeing itself from the vicissitudes of sexual schizophrenia, a psychoanalyst thought it was an ordinary twinning process which had been delayed by a severe case of prenatal sibling rivalry. When the split was complete, two thin Ian Nicols lay together on the bed.

The resentment each felt for the other had not been foreseen or guarded against. In bed the original Ian Nicol could be recognised by his position (he lay on the right of the bed) but as soon as both men were strong enough to walk each claimed ownership of birth certificate, union card, clothes, wife and National Insurance benefit. One day in the hospital grounds they started fighting. They were evenly matched and there are conflicting opinions about who won. On leaving hospital they took legal action against each other for theft of identity. The case was resolved by a medical examination which showed that one of them had no navel.

The second Ian Nicol changed his name by deed poll and is now called Macbeth. Sometimes he and Ian Nicol write to each other. The latest news is that each has a bald patch on the back of his head.

SO NEAR

Ruth Wishart

IN THE COURSE of 1984 Scottish Opera mounted a rather controversial production of *Turandot*. For some weeks arguments raged in the letters page of the press as to its artistic merit. Latterly it went on tour to Edinburgh where, in the first week, the company managed to notch up just 79 advance bookings. A columnist in the Glasgow *Evening Times* gleefully hugged this intelligence to his stout West of Scotland heart. There you are, he told his readers, Glasgow can muster more letters to the press about opera than Edinburgh can ticket holders.

What he was suggesting of course was that despite the internationally acclaimed three-week Kulturfest Edinburgh mounts in the summer, its citizenry's claim to be Scotland's premier arts lovers is somewhat spurious.

And it is.

The kind of music Edinburgh makes most prolifically is mouth music. It talks a fine game about an opera house and twenty years later bemused tourists can still have their attention drawn to the hole in the ground in Castle Terrace which was originally to be the site.

But Glasgow, unfashionable gritty old Glasgow, did build an opera house. Or, more practically, it put together a deal whereby the old Theatre Royal, formerly part of the Scottish Television complex, was able to revert to a theatre which was then redecorated in the grand manner.

A concert hall is scheduled to follow by the end of the decade. Glasgow is also the home of the Scottish National Orchestra, you see, and Scottish Ballet. And in 1983 it added to its renowned main museum and art gallery the stunning sandstone, glass and pine home for the Burrell Collection in Pollok Park.

(Did I perhaps forget to mention that Glasgow is unrivalled in Europe for scope and variety of parkland?)

Keep Glasgow Tidy

(Or that it now has its own small but perfectly formed festival known as Mayfest and celebrated for two weeks in that month?)

Let me say at this juncture that, yes, I suffer from ingrained bias and no, I am not working for Glasgow's George Square Tourist Bureau. But I happily would. Nothing gives the unreconstructed Glaswegian more pleasure than helping guests to find out for themselves that the city's new slogan "Glasgow's Miles Better" is actually true. Honest!

The morning this slogan was exported to London accompanied by the kind of five-course Scottish breakfast only ever eaten by Japanese businessmen, the former Lord Provost of Glasgow admitted people accosted him in the street demanding to know "Miles better than What?" "Than it used to be," he retorted defiantly.

And with its newly sandblasted tenements, the rebirth of the city centre—real folks actually live there now—and the restoration and rehabilitation of some of its most famous old buildings it would take an Edinburgh man to deny it.

Which brings us back to the thorny business of the Glasgow-Edinburgh divide. Forty-four miles distant geographically, Georgian Edinburgh and Victorian Glasgow are different in just about every way possible. It's partly a question of attitude. The Israelis have a word for the quality of cheeky brassneckedness. They call it a *chutzpah* and it translates in Glaswegian as gallus.

There is no Edinburgh equivalent. Edinburgh folks don't get gallus, at least not in public, not on Sundays and never in front of the children. It would be iniquitous to perpetuate the bad old joke that Edinburgh dwellers are less than hospitable in the matter of inviting you for a meal, but there is nevertheless a lack of generosity in their spirit. In Edinburgh you get the feeling that good humour and *joie de vivre* require to be rationed—otherwise who knows what might happen? They might have a good time two nights running for heavens' sakes!

Like a substantial number of Glaswegians, I spend a very great deal of time in Edinburgh during the Festival there. It's usually a marvellous three weeks and one of the reasons is that the city becomes truly cosmopolitan. Not to put too fine a point on it, the native Edinburgh hordes are diluted by a wide cross-section of visitors.

No city could be expected to maintain a carnival atmosphere on an all-year-round basis, but few cities revert to type quite so disappointingly as Scotland's capital when the final note from the piper is heard on the last evening of the Tattoo. (The Tattoo is not, of course anything to do with the Festival—*far* too downmarket and lots of punters in the audience. Edinburgh has punters too and tries hard to pretend otherwise.)

Glasgow made some horrendous postwar mistakes in its housing policy which left it with a series of peripheral housing estates appallingly planned, depressingly designed, and completely lacking any kind of facilities which might have given them a heart and a community status. We know that now. Edinburgh did too, but Edinburgh rarely allows itself publicly to agonise about Pilton and Craigmillar because Edinburgh would prefer not to acknowledge that the Athens of the North can boast some slums as well as magnificent terraces.

Edinburgh of course is a beautiful town. A much prettier place altogether than Glasgow; a city that is quite breathtaking to walk round on a fine sunny day with the buildings and the skylines showing their best profile. It's a fine city to visit and that is what I do with it.

But to stay there? To have to get a train to Glasgow when in dire need of a belly-laugh?

To have to put on matching pieces of clothing to go shopping?

Edinburgh is quite frankly too much of an ordeal to live up to.

But let us be fair and concede that if the average Glaswegian has no notion to take the Orient Express from Queen Street to Waverley, then the average Edinburgher would just as soon he didn't. Edinburgh folks think Glasgow folk are not merely common but downright ignorant with it. Edinburgh folk think Glasgow folk imagine the Royal Mile is the Rose Street pub crawl.

Edinburgh folk are surprised not merely that Glaswegians know which knife and fork to use, but that they have been trained to use eating implements at all.

This I well know because I have an Edinburgh auntie who comes to the Wild West when any of the family is to be cremated and wears a hat to ensure that they are dispatched with proper formality. She well knows that her place in heaven is secure, since she has committed no significant earthly sin since the age of five.

But there is no trace of envy within my mortal soul since it's a pound to a pinch of snuff that Heaven will be stiff with other folks' Edinburgh aunties too.

It's got to take the edge off Paradise.

Ideas above their station

WATCH YOUR LANGUAGE

Janey Buchan

WRITE A CHAPTER for a book on Glasgow? What kind of Glasgow are we talking about? For me Glasgow is the city of class and, above all else, the city of language. Not that kind of language—though sometimes that too—but its command of a kind of interpretation of the English language allied to a strongly literal view of life. That it also spills over into its political life is evident. No chance of you getting a big head in Glasgow politics—there are always plenty of punters around who'll quickly cut you down to size.

Even if a Glasgow accent was not immediately recognisable—whether of the Kelvinside or Partick ends—there are also clear grammatical ways of Glaswegianese. For example, the player or, more frequently, the manager who says to the radio or TV commentator, "We have went to a great deal of trouble..." or, "We've did exactly what the boss told us . . ."

This often comes from someone who is reasonably well read, not a fool, and yet doesn't relate his spoken language to anything he reads. I know at least one grammarian who thinks that the foregoing is quite acceptable and has great strength. He'll need to go out and fight that one for himself.

Perhaps it is the comfort that this language of our own gives us that makes us cling the more tenaciously to it. For we do have a way of communicating with each other that must, from time to time, be as foreign to someone from Falkirk as it is to someone from Famagusta. But it is immediately recognisable to ourselves and who else matters? We don't have to make tortuous explanations when we grasp this.

The kind of "in"-ness that I mean is exemplified by the night when Peter Meldrum, then Lord Provost of Glasgow, was facing a studio audience at STV on Glasgow and its problems. Inevitably the studio audience availed themselves of the opportunity to give voice to their own complaints. The discussion reached housing and the Corporation's system of allocation. Peter was doing his best when this elderly woman intervened and said, "Well, if that's true what you're saying—why was I allowed to overcrowd masel'?" Every Glaswegian in the audience or sitting at home knew precisely what she meant but I wondered what on earth anyone else made of it. The sight of poor Peter's crumpled face showed the difficulty he had, let alone anyone else.

It shows up too when we live in the world that is Glasgow and *only* Glasgow. A friend of ours was, during the war, given the job of fighting any desert oil-fires that broke out. The system was that there were several people with the necessary skills and their whereabouts were always known so that they could be dragged out at a moment's notice and flown to the appropriate spot. Our friend went out to the newly arrived squad, saw a couple of new faces and one of them was clearly a Scot. "You're Scottish?" "Aye." "Where from?" "Soothside." Not a moment's hesitation to think that you could come from anywhere else but Glasgow and not a moment's concession either that South of the river is the *only* place to come from. The cry should not be "No Surrender" but "Nae Concessions".

It follows therefore that everyone who does not immediately comprehend us or who writes in the school text-book style of the English language is some kind of poor soul (pronounced sowel as in bowel).

The most telling example of this happened to me personally. I was on top of a bus and we had stopped outside Tiffany's ballroom (really the Locarno or "The Loc"), waiting on a relief driver. Two women were chatting and it was impossible not to listen to their conversation. Suddenly one of them said, "Wid ye look at that—the stupit," and when we all looked we knew that she was referring to a window bill in Pullar's dry-cleaning shop which said, "Hire an electric carpet shampoo-er here". "I'nt that no ridiculous? Who the hell's got electric carpets?" There was a marvellous moment when everyone's head tipped forward slightly and yet no one actually laughed out loud. Of course it should be a lesson for every advertising copy-writer—watch your English when it's aimed at literal-minded Glaswegians.

In sport this language of ours is a great benefit. When it is linked to the keen/satirical/cynical knowledge of politics it is devastating. My brother came

No politics, please, we're keelies

home for Hogmanay long years ago. He went to a game at Shawfield and a lone player in the middle of the field rose very gracefully to head a ball and the ball flew way over his head. The crowd groaned and a loud voice said, "Aw—away back tae the fuckin' Bolshoi". The current political stushie at the time was some crisis over whether the Bolshoi could or could not come to Britain for a tour.

It is a small step from the world of Glasgow sport to the world of Glasgow politics and at the time of my marriage—November 1945—the first visit to Britain of the famous Moscow Dynamo was on. They came to Glasgow to play Rangers but en route had beaten Cardiff City 10-0, and had a row with Arsenal who were accused of signing in too quickly some England internationals. They declared therefore that all future teams had to be approved by them before kick-off. The indignation in those days that anyone even dared to *think* of telling Rangers anything . . . well.

Rangers were genuinely then about to sign Caskie, a Scottish internationalist from Liverpool. The Russians looked at the list and said, "No Caskie. No internationalist brought in . . ." etc. etc. Before the day of the match the Russians were taken on the then obligatory trip doon the watter (Mid-November too! What hospitality to offer anyone!). As they passed the Blythswood yard there were ships at an early stage of building. A banner was strung between them which read, "Who's afraid of wee Jimmy Caskie?" and when we think of the size of Caskie and the size of the members of Dynamo it was a classic Glasgow shout.

On the day of the game itself when we got to the crowd there were great examples of welcoming Glasgow graffiti, "Good old Rangers. Hammer and sicken them!" On a personal note I have to say that when the first Dynamo goal was scored, *very* early in the game, I laughed rather a lot. The second goal, some minutes later, really set me off (like all true Glaswegians there is nothing funnier to me than the great and the good on a banana skin). The silence around me was deafening and a wee man in front turned and growled to my husband of three days, "Hey! You! tell your ----ing wumman it's no' ----ing funny". The menace was clear and my husband and our best man pleaded, "Try not to do that again"

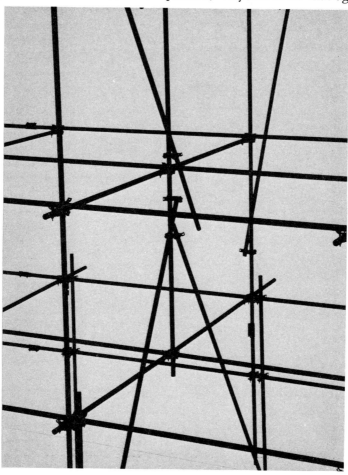

Which way up does it go?

Six years after the game when all but the most devoted *aficianados* had forgotten the background at least there was a General Election and a friend of ours, a strong, witty, academic woman was out canvassing in Shettleston. A man came to the door wearing only his semmit. She was a bit taken aback and, keeping her eyes suitably raised to his face, and above, said, "I'm here about the General Election . . . and it's very important that people use their vote." The man interrupted, "I know all that. I know that. Who are you from?" She said, "Well, actually I'm from the Communist Party." "The Communists," he yelled. "Me vote for them? Them that widnae let Caskie play?" Six years of the Cold War only meant this long forgotten insult to Glasgow.

The knowledge of Left politics is of a reasonable standard. My one time MP, Neil Carmichael, was once working on a site as an engineer and heard some workmen watching a mate slip a three-foot piece of copper piping down his trouser leg and saying, "Ye gonny lift that?" (note "lift" rather than "pinch"). "Och, it's only a wee bit of the bosses' surplus value," he replied. Today's arid "Marxists" would never have a command of language comprising the true Glaswegian and the near true Marxist definition of class like that.

In the days when Glasgow was one of the few cities in Britain, if not the only one, that allowed you to "chalk the streets"—i.e. write or, illegally, paint political slogans and notices of political meetings, on street ends—a friend of ours, Andy McLerie, a great political wit on the Left in Glasgow, arrived at the CP rooms, having observed on every street end in Govan the slogan, "Hands off Cypress", when the Makarios crisis was at its height. He moaned at them in mock horror, "Christ—they'll think it's the Tree Lovers' Society that's been oot."

If you doubt this thesis on the strength and individuality of Glasgow's language then try this test. Write down every phrase you know to describe a disagreeable/moaning person in Glasgow's language and then write down those that are more commonly known throughout the UK. Then it will be true—Glasgow's miles better. Who can beat:

He/she's got a face like a hauf-chewed caramel
He/she's got a face like the wrang end o' a bus
He/she's got a face like the end o' a Belfast ham.
A torn face
He/she's got a face like a torn melodeon wi' the tune hingin' oot
or when we move on to intelligence—or lack of it
He's got these weans' heids fillt full a mince (of a greatly disliked Sunday school teacher)
His heid's full o' wee trains
His/hers . . .

Look, why the hell am I bothering wi' all this? Away an' finish the lot for yoursels.